THE STUDY OF COMMEMORATIVE COINS FROM 1964 TO 2022

COMMEMORATIVE COINS OF INDIA

SATYAJIT BALIYARSINGH

ISBN 979-8-88833-698-4

CONTENTS

MINTING HISTORY OF COINS

The first coins seems to be Lydian's of 600 BC a kingdom of ancient Greece head of a lion is seem on the coin which made of electrum, an alloy of gold & silver. It was minted by ALYETTES of Lydian (610-560 BC)

A king of the mermnad dynasty in Lydia the son of sadyattes & gradson of Ardys.

The most interesting fact that alyattes was the first monarch who issued coins made from electrum & his successor Croesus was the first to issue gold coin in the world history.

When Sher Shah Suri took control of the Mugal empire in the year 1540 then he introduced the coin named as DAM (a small copper coin) which was forst introduced & then introduced mohur the gold coin & rupiya the silver coin later Mughal standardized silver (Rupiya) & gold & Mohur) in order ot consolidate the monetary system of India. a rupee was divided in to 40 DAMS (1540-1545)

- ➢ 1 Anna-125,548,000 coins minted from (1918 to 1940) in copper nickel.
- ➢ 1 Quarter Anna-1,681, 276, 200, coin minted from (1912 to 1936)

When in the year 1934 the reserve bank of India (Act 1934) which was passed to manage currency in India & derives its role in currency management by the RBI act since then the general circulation of coins where introduced after along in the year 1964, the first commemorative coins of Jawaharlal Nehru was minted in Bombay mint with a circulation of 1 rupees & 50 Paise & with the bust of Jawaharlal Nehru.

Commemorative coins are that where issue to commemorate recall & show respect for someone or something some particular event birth or death centenary of famous personalities or an recently died, commemoration of special government programs or sport events anniversaries of historical incidents government organization etc.

MINTING SYMBOLS ON INDIAN COINS

Sign	Metals
Ab	Aluminium-Bronze Copper-92 5, Aluminium-6 % & Nickel-2 %
Am	Aluminium-Magnesium Magnesium-3.5 To 4 5 Remainder Aluminum
B	Bronze Copper-97 %, Zinc-2.5 % & Nickel-25 %
Cn	Cupro-Nickel Copper-75 % & Nickel-25 %
Ccn	Outer Ring-Alu-Bronze Copper-92 %, Aluminium-6 % & Nickel-2 % Central Piece-Cupro Nickel Copper-75 % & Nickel-25 %
N	Nickel 9 100 % Pure Nickel)
Nb	Nickel-Bronze Copper-75 %, Zinc-20 5, Nickel-5 %
S80	Silver-80 % Copper-20 %
S92	Silver-92.5 % Copper-7.5 %
S50	Quaternary –Alloy Silver-50 %,Copper-40 %, Nickel-5 % & Zinc-5 %
Ss	Ferritic Stainless Steel Iron-82 %, Chromium-18 %

HISTORY ON INDIAN CURRENCY (FROM MUGHALS TO AFTER INDEPENDENCE)

First battle of Panipat (1526) BABER defeated IBRAHIM LODHI and established mugal rule in DELHI. This was the big event in the history and also establishing the new empire in order to make the event memories he introduced silver coins in the year 1526 and continued till 1530 and named it as Silver Tankas or Shahrukhi (4 grams). After BABER his son HUMAYUN became the new Mughal king but SHERSHAH SURI defeated HUMAYUN in the battle of CHAUSA, then shershah suri started the ruling Delhi. Sher Shah Suri did not like the silver Tanka of the Mughals then the order his (manuscript to design a new model of coin when the saw the coin Sher Shah Suri said Rupaiah (A beautiful Art). So now from Tanka is replaced bu Rupaiah which come automatically from his mouth. Then the TANKA of mugals was replaced by rupaiah.

It continued to be the standard under later Mughal rules & even the british who used the term 'rupee' for silver coins & set their might close to sher shahs coins at 11 gms.

After Sher Shah Suri when Akbar ruled Delhi the continued with rupaiah and introduced Asharfi mohur which was minted in gold. it was used for special purpose but for Arm trading rupaiah was used. Akbar also experimented with the shape of coins such as (circular, square and polygonal) hence the polygonal shape is well known by its name Mehrabi.

Akbar preached about Din-i-ilahi, and this is very well visible through the coin introduced during his reign according to the month name as Din-i-illahi Farbadi, kardart, when Jahangir became king in the year 1605, in his code he had Persian poet, as he has a liking for poet so he printed poet on coins. As he was also interested in astrology so zodiac sign was also seen on the coins.

The Coin released in the name of Nur-Jahan as the 20th Queen of Jahangir. After that again he released a coin with his own portrait, as in Islam to take picture is a crime, as it was a big issue of that time many people criticized it. This coin (Jahngir Protrait Coin) was given as the special gifts which they can were on their turbans or Sashes to show that day had been graced by Imperial favor.

When Shah Jahan (1628-1658) ruled he ordered the melting of Jahangir's Portrait and Zodiac coins this is what makes the rare surviving specimens so precious. Hardly there are some limited coins which nearly cost will be around 40-50 Lakhs.

Hence from this Period The thinking of commemorative coin was introduce but after independence in the year 1964 the Birth Anniversary of Jawaharlal Nehru was portrait on the coin to commemorate this event as memorable from this coin commemorative coin era begins till now.

JAWAHARLAL NEHRU
(1889-1964)

Date of Issue: 14th November 1964

OBVERSE DESCRIPTION OF COIN

Ashok lion Capital with Value of one Rupees Below, Mint mark below value & India/Bharat on Top half and Rupees/Rupaya in bottom half.

REVERSE DESCRIPTION OF COIN

Bust of Jawaharlal Nehru facing Left, Date 1889-1964 Below

Sl No	Year	Denomina-tion	Weight of the Coin	Metal Compositions	Shape & Size			Mint
					Dia	Edge	Shape	
1	1964	1 Rupee	10 Gms	100% Nickel	28 Mm	Milled, S.e, Serr.200	Circular	Mumbai
2	1964	50 Paisa	5 Gms	100% Nickel	24 Mm	Milled, S.e., Serr.150	Circular	Mumbai

MAHATMA GANDHI
(1869-1948)

Date of Issue: 2nd OCTOBER 1969

OBVERSE DESCRIPTION OF COIN

Ashoka Lion Capital, denomination below,
Centennial-Birth of Mahatma Gandhi

REVERSE DESCRIPTION OF COIN

Bust of Mahatma Gandhi facing left

Sl No	Year	Denomi-nation	Weight of the Coin	Metal Composi-tions	Shape & Size			Mint
					Dia	Edge	Shape	
1	1969	10 Rupee	15 Gms	80 % Ag, 20% Cu	34 Mm	Milled, Serr.155	Circular	Mumbai
2	1969	1 Rupee	10 Gms	Pure Nickel	28 Mm	Milled, Serr.200	Circular	Mumbai
3	1969	50 Paise	5 Gms	Pure Nickel	24 Mm	Milled, S.e., Serr.150	Circular	Mumbai
4	1969	20 Paise	4.5 Gms	Alminium Bronze	22 Mm	Milled, Serr.112	Circular	Mumbai

FOOD FOR ALL
(1970)

Date of Issue: 16th OCTOBER 1970

OBVERSE DESCRIPTION OF COIN

Ashoka Lion Capital, denomination below

REVERSE DESCRIPTION OF COIN

Floating lotus flower below sun, flanked by wheat grains
B (letter "B") = Mumbai Proof Issues *Lettering:* 1971

Sl No	Year	Denomi-nation	Weight of the Coin	Metal Composi-tions	Shape & Size			Mint
					Dia	Edge	Shape	
1	1970	10 Rupee	15 Gms	80 % Ag, 20% Cu	34 Mm	Milled, Serr.155	Circular	Mumbai
2	1970	20 Paise	4.5 Gms	Aluminium Bronze	22 Mm	Milled, Serr.112	Circular	Mumbai

25th ANNIVERSARY OF INDIA'S INDEPENDENCE (1972)

Date of Issue:15th AUGUST 1972

OBVERSE DESCRIPTION OF COIN

Asoka lion pedestal, denomination below

REVERSE DESCRIPTION OF COIN

Figures with Indian flag, parliament building in background(small dot/diamond) = Mumbai, Mumbai Proof Issues= Calcutta *Lettering* 1947-1972

Sl No	Year	Denomi-nation	Weight of the Coin	Metal Composi-tions	Shape & Size			Mint
					Dia	Edge	Shape	
1	1972	10 Rupee	22.5 Gms	Quaternary Allloy	39 Mm	Milled, Serr 180	Circular	Mumbai
2	1972	50 Paisa	5 Gms	Nickel	24 Mm	Milled, S.e., Serr.205	Circular	Mumbai

GROW MORE FOOD
(1973)

Date of Issue: 15th AUGUST 1973

OBVERSE DESCRIPTION OF COIN
Asoka lion pedestal, denomination below

REVERSE DESCRIPTION OF COIN
Inscription on shield within grain stalks

Sl No	Year	Denomi-nation	Weight of the Coin	Metal Com-positions	Shape & Size			Mint
					Dia	Edge	Shape	
1	1973	20 Rupee	30 Gms	Quaternary Allloy	44 Mm	Milled, Serr.200	Circular	Mumbai
2	1973	10 Rupee	22.5 Gms	Quaternary Allloy	39 Mm	Milled, Serr.180	Circular	Mumbai
3	1973	50 Paise	5 Gm	Cupro Nickel	24 Mm	Milled, S.e., Serr.205	Circular	Mumbai

PLANNED FAMILIES FOOD FOR ALL (1974)

Date of Issue: 15th August 1974

OBVERSE DESCRIPTION OF COIN

The Ashoka Lion Capital, Denomination Below, Bharat /India on sides

REVERSE DESCRIPTION OF COIN

Family within triangle, grain stalks and boath sides, Date below 197, Legend:PLANNED FAMILIES:FOOD FOR ALL1974

Sl No	Year	Denomi-nation	Weight of the Coin	Metal Com-positions	Shape & Size			Mint
					Dia	Edge	Shape	
1	1974	50 Rupee	35 Gms	Quaternary Allloy	44 Mm	Milled, Serr.200	Circular	Mumbai
2	1974	10 Rupees	25 Gms	Cupro Nickel	39 Mm	Milled, Serr.180	Circular	Mumbai
3	1974	10 Paise	2.30 Gms	Aluminium Magnesium	26 Mm	Unmilled	12 Scallops	Mumbai

EQUALITY, DEVELOPMENT, PEACE (1975)

Date of Issue: 15 AUGUST 1975

OBVERSE DESCRIPTION OF COIN

The Ashoka Lion Capital, Denomination Below, Bharat /India on sides

REVERSE DESCRIPTION OF COIN

Bust of women on left with grain stalks at right, date on both sides-1975, *legend:* EQUALITY DEVELOPMENT PEACE

Sl No	Year	Denomi-nation	Weight of the Coin	Metal Com-positions	Shape & Size			Mint
					Dia	Edge	Shape	
1	1975	50 Rupee	35 Gms	Quaternary Allloy	44 Mm	Milled, Serr.200	Circular	Mumbai
2	1975	10 Rupees	25 Gms	Cupro Nickel	39 Mm	Milled, Serr.180	Circular	Mumbai
3	1975	10 Paise	2.30 Gms	Aluminium Magnesium	26 Mm	Unmilled	12 Scallops	Mumbai

FOOD & WORK FOR ALL
(1976)

Date of Issue: 15 AUGUST 1976

OBVERSE DESCRIPTION OF COIN
The Ashoka Lion Capital, Denomination Below, Bharat /India on sides

REVERSE DESCRIPTION OF COIN
People on tractor, utility pool, Building at back side, date on both sides-1976, *legend:* food & work for all

Sl No	Year	Denom-ination	Weight of the Coin	Metal Com-positions	Shape & Size			Mint
					Dia	Edge	Shape	
1	1976	50 Rupee	35 Gms	Quaternary Allloy	44 Mm	Milled, Serr.200	Circular	Mumbai
2	1976	10 Rupees	25 Gms	Cupro Nickel	39 Mm	Milled, Serr.180	Circular	Mumbai
3	1976	10 Paise	2.30 Gms	Aluminium Magnesium	26 Mm	Unmilled	12 Scallops	Mumbai
4	1976	5 Paise	1.5 Gms	Aluminium Magnesium	22/19 Mm	Unmilled	Sq With Rounded Corners	Mumbai

SAVE FOR DEVELOPMENT
(1977)

Date of Issue: 15th AUGUST 1977

OBVERSE DESCRIPTION OF COIN

The Ashoka Lion Capital, Denomination Below, Bharat /India on sides

REVERSE DESCRIPTION OF COIN

Symbols of development, Factory health and education, Building in Background Date Below-1977, *legend:* "save for development"

Sl No	Year	Denomination	Weight of the Coin	Metal Compositions	Shape & Size			Mint
					Dia	Edge	Shape	
1	1977	50 Rupee	35 Gms	Quaternary Allloy	44 Mm	Milled, Serr.200	Circular	Mumbai
2	1977	10 Rupees	25 Gms	Cupro Nickel	39 Mm	Milled, Serr.180	Circular	Mumbai
3	1977	10 Paise	2.30 Gms	Aluminium Magnesium	26 Mm	Unmilled	12 Scallops	Mumbai
4	1977	5 Paise	1.5 Gms	Aluminium Magnesium	22/19 Mm	Unmilled	Sq With Rounded Corners	Mumbai

FOOD AND SHELTER FOR ALL
(1978)

Date of Issue: 15ᵗʰ AUGUST 1978

OBVERSE DESCRIPTION OF COIN

The Ashoka Lion Capital, Denomination Below, Bharat /India on sides

REVERSE DESCRIPTION OF COIN

Grain stalk, House and Road, Date Mention above:1978, Legend "food and shelter for all"

Sl No	Year	Denomination	Weight of the Coin	Metal Compositions	Shape & Size			Mint
					Dia	Edge	Shape	
1	1978	50 Rupee	35 Gms	Quaternary Allloy	44 Mm	Milled, Serr.200	Circular	Mumbai
2	1978	10 Rupee	25 Gms	Cupro Nickel	39 Mm	Milled, Serr.180	Circular	Mumbai
3	1978	10 Paise	2.30 Gms	Aluminium Magnesium	26 Mm	Unmilled	12 Scallops	Mumbai
4	1978	5 Paise	1.5 Gms	Aluminium Magnesium	22/19 Mm	Unmilled	Sq With Rounded Corners	Mumbai

HAPPY CHILD NATION'S PRIDE
(1979)

Date of Issue: 15th AUGUST 1979

OBVERSE DESCRIPTION OF COIN

The Ashoka Lion Capital, Denomination Below, Bharat /India on sides

REVERSE DESCRIPTION OF COIN

Logo of international year of the Child, Date below: 1979, legend: Happy child nation's pride.

Sl No	Year	De-nomi-nation	Weight of the Coin	Metal Com-positions	Shape & Size			Mint
					Dia	Edge	Shape	
1	1979	50 Rupee	35 Gms	Quaternary Allloy	44 Mm	Milled, Serr.200	Circular	Mumbai
2	1979	10 Rupees	25 Gms	Cupro Nickel	39 Mm	Milled, Serr.180	Circular	Mumbai
3	1979	10 Paise	2.30 Gms	Aluminium Magnesium	26 Mm Across Scallopes	Unmilled	12 Scallops	Mumbai
4	1979	5 Paise	1.5 Gms	Aluminium Magnesium	22/19 Mm	Unmilled	Sq With Rounded Corners	Mumbai

RURAL WOMEN'S ADVANCEMENT (1980)

Date of Issue:01ˢᵗ JANUARY 1981

OBVERSE DESCRIPTION OF COIN

The Ashoka Lion Capital, Denomination Below, Bharat /India on sides

REVERSE DESCRIPTION OF COIN

Women Using Electric Grain Husking machine, Date Below: 1980
Legend: Rural Women's Advancement 1980

SI No	Year	Denom-ination	Weight of the Coin	Metal Com-positions	Shape & Size			Mint
					Dia	Edge	Shape	
1	1980	100 Rupees	35 Gms	Quaternary Allloy	44 Mm	Milled, Serr.200	Circular	Mumbai
2	1980	10 Rupees	25 Gms	Cupro Nickel	39 Mm	Milled, Serr.180	Circular	Mumbai
3	1980	25 Paise	2.50 Gms	Cupro Nickel	19 Mm	Milled, Serr.100	Circular	Mumbai
4	1980	10 Paise	2.30 Gms	Aluminium Magnesium	26 Mm Across Scallopes	Unmilled	12 Scallops	Mumbai

WORLD FOOD DAY
(1981)

Date of Issue: 16th OCTOBER 1981

OBVERSE DESCRIPTION OF COIN

Ashoka Lion Capital, denomination below Six double headed arrows around border

REVERSE DESCRIPTION OF COIN

Man with corn sheaf, women with basket of fruits, date below-1981, legend "world food day"

Sl No	Year	Denomi-nation	Weight of the Coin	Metal Com-positions	Shape & Size			Mint
					Dia	Edge	Shape	
1	1981	100 Rupees	35 Gms	Quaternary Allloy	44 Mm	Milled, Serr.200	Circular	Mumbai
2	1981	10 Rupees	25 Gms	Cupro Nickel	39 Mm	Milled, Serr.180	Circular	Mumbai
3	1981	25 Paise	2.50 Gms	Cupro Nickel	19 Mm	Milled, Serr.100	Circular	Mumbai
4	1981	10 Paise	2.30 Gms	Aluminium Magnesium	26 Mm Across Scallopes	Unmilled	12 Scallops	Mumbai

INTERNATIONAL YEAR OF THE CHILD (1981)

Date of Issue: 1981

OBVERSE DESCRIPTION OF COIN

Asoka lion capital, denomination below, Bharat/India on sides

REVERSE DESCRIPTION OF COIN

Musicians and dancer Date below: 1981, legend "international year of the child"

SI No	Year	Denom-ination	Weight of the Coin	Metal Compo-sitions	Shape & Size			Mint
					Dia	Edge	Shape	
1	1981	100 Rupees	29.16 Gms	Sterling Silver	44 Mm	Milled, Serr.200	Circular	Mumbai
2	1981	100 Rupees	58.32 Gms	Sterling Silver	44 Mm	Milled, Serr.150	Circular	Mumbai

WORLD FOOD DAY
(1982)

Date of Issue:1982

OBVERSE DESCRIPTION OF COIN
Asoka lion capital, denomination below, Bharat/India on sides

REVERSE DESCRIPTION OF COIN
Grain spring within stylized sun design Legend "World Food day" with year "1982"

Sl No	Year	Denomination	Weight of the Coin	Metal Compositions	Shape & Size			Mint
					Dia	Edge	Shape	
1	1982	10 Paisa	1.75 Gms	Sterling Silver	23 Mm	Milled, Serr.200	Scalloped	Kolkata
2	1982	20 Paisa	2.2 Gms	Sterling Silver	26 Mm	Milled, Serr.150	Hexagonal	Kolkata

IX ASIAN GAMES DELHI
(1982)

Date of Issue: 19th NOVEMBER 1982

OBVERSE DESCRIPTION OF COIN
Asoka lion capital, denomination below, Bharat/India on sides

REVERSE DESCRIPTION OF COIN
Sun Above, IX Asian Games Logo, Date below: 1982 Legend: IX Asian Games

SI No	Year	Denomination	Weight of the Coin	Metal Compositions	Shape & Size			Mint
					Dia	Edge	Shape	
1	1982	100 Rupees	35 Gms	Quaternary Allloy	44 Mm	Milled, Serr.200	Circular	Mumbai
2	1982	10 Rupees	25 Gms	Cupro Nickel	39 Mm	Milled, Serr.180	Circular	Mumbai
3	1982	2 Rupees	2.50 Gms	Cupro Nickel	28 Mm	Milled, Serr.100	Circular	Mumbai
4	1982	50 Paise	2.30 Gms	Aluminium Magnesium	26 Mm Across Scallopes	Unmilled	12 Scallops	Mumbai

NATIONAL INTEGRATION
(1982)

Date of Issue: DECEMBER 1982

OBVERSE DESCRIPTION OF COIN
Asoka lion capital, denomination below, Bharat/India on sides

REVERSE DESCRIPTION OF COIN
Map of India with Date below=1982 legend = national integration.

Sl No	Year	Denomination	Weight of the Coin	Metal Compositions	Shape & Size			Mint
					Dia	Edge	Shape	
1	1982	100 Rupees	35 Gms	Quaternary Allloy	44 Mm	Milled, Serr.200	Circular	Kolkata
2	1982	10 Rupees	25 Gms	Cupro Nickel	39 Mm	Milled, Serr.180	Circular	Kolkata
3	1982	2 Rupees	8 Gms	Cupro Nickel	28 Mm	Milled, S.e Serr.200	Circular	Kolkata
4	1982	50 Paise	5 Gms	Cupro Nickel	24 Mm	Milled, S.e Serr.205	Circular	Kolkata

FISHERIES – WORLD FOOD DAY (1982)

Date of Issue: 1983

OBVERSE DESCRIPTION OF COIN
Asoka lion capital, denomination below, Bharat/India on sides

REVERSE DESCRIPTION OF COIN
People with fishing nets Legends: Fisheries with year "1983" above.

SI No	Year	Denom-ination	Weight of the Coin	Metal Com-positions	Shape & Size			Mint
					Dia	Edge	Shape	
1	1983	20 Paise	2.2 Gms	Aluminium	26 Mm	Milled, Serr.200	Hexognal	Kolkata

RBI GOLDEN JUBILEE (1985)

Date of Issue: 19th NOVEMBER 1985

OBVERSE DESCRIPTION OF COIN

Asoka lion capital, denomination below, Bharat/India on sides

REVERSE DESCRIPTION OF COIN

Tiger with palm tree, crest of RBI, Date below 1935-85, Legend –"Reserve Bank of India" Golden Jubilee.

Sl No	Year	Denomi-nation	Weight of the Coin	Metal Com-positions	Shape & Size			Mint
					Dia	Edge	Shape	
1	1985	100 Rupees	35 Gms	Quaternary Allloy	44 Mm	Milled, Serr.200	Circular	Mumbai
2	1985	10 Ru-pees	25 Gms	Cupro Nickel	39 Mm	Milled, Serr.180	Circular	Mumbai
3	1985	2 Rupees	12.5 Gms	Cupro Nickel	31 Mm	Milled, Serr. 150	Circular	Mumbai
4	1985	50 Paise	5 Gms	Cupro Nickel	24 Mm	Milled, S.e Serr.205	Circular	Mumbai

HOMAGE TO INDIRA GANDHI
(1917-1984)

Date of Issue: APRIL 1985

OBVERSE DESCRIPTION OF COIN
Asoka lion capital, denomination below, Bharat/India on sides

REVERSE DESCRIPTION OF COIN
Bust of Indira Gandhi Date below 1917-1984
Legend: INDIRA GANDHI

SI No	Year	De-nomi-nation	Weight of the Coin	Metal Com-positions	Shape & Size			Mint
					Dia	Edge	Shape	
1	1985	100 Rupees	35 Gms	Quaternary Allloy	44 Mm	Milled, Serr.200	Circular	Mumbai
2	1985	20 Rupees	25 Gms	Cupro Nickel	39 Mm	Milled, Serr.180	Circular	Mumbai
3	1985	5 Rupees	12.5 Gms	Cupro Nickel	31 Mm	Milled, Serr. 150	Circular	Mumbai
4	1985	50 Paise	5 Gms	Cupro Nickel	24 Mm	Milled, S.e Serr.205	Circular	Mumbai

INTERNATIONAL YOUTH YEAR
(1985)

Date of Issue: 06th November 1985

OBVERSE DESCRIPTION OF COIN
Asoka lion capital, denomination below, Bharat/India on sides

REVERSE DESCRIPTION OF COIN
Dove and Laurel Branch, Date above, Legend "International Youth Year"

SI No	Year	Denomination	Weight of the Coin	Metal Compositions	Shape & Size			Mint
					Dia	Edge	Shape	
1	1985	100 Rupees	35	S50	44	Milled /200	Circular	Calcutta
2	1985	10 Rupees	25	Cupro Nickel	39	Milled /200	Circular	Calcutta
3	1985	1 Rupees	6	Cupro Nickel	26	Security Edge /204	Circular	Calcutta

FISHERIES WORLD FOOD DAY
(1986)

Date of Issue: 19th JANUARY 1987

OBVERSE DESCRIPTION OF COIN
Asoka lion capital, denomination below, Bharat/India on sides

REVERSE DESCRIPTION OF COIN
People with fishing nets, Date above 1986. Legend= "Fishires FAO

Sl No	Year	Denomina-tion	Weight of the Coin	Metal Com-positions	Shape & Size			Mint
					Dia	Edge	Shape	
1	1986	100 Rupees	35 Gms	Quaternary Allloy	44 Mm	Milled, Serr.200	Circular	Mumbai
2	1986	20 Rupees	25 Gms	Cupro Nickel	39 Mm	Milled, Serr.180	Circular	Mumbai
3	1986	50 Paise	5 Gms	Cupro Nickel	24 Mm	Milled, S.e Serr.205	Circular	Mumbai

SMALL FARMERS
(1987)

Date of Issue: 16th OCTOBER 1987

OBVERSE DESCRIPTION OF COIN

Asoka lion capital, denomination below, Bharat/India on sides

REVERSE DESCRIPTION OF COIN

Farmer transplanting crop, Date below-1987, Legend "small farmers"

Sl No	Year	Denomina-tion	Weight of the Coin	Metal Com-positions	Shape & Size			Mint
					Dia	Edge	Shape	
1	1987	100 Rupees	35 Gms	Quaternary Allloy	44 Mm	Milled, Serr.200	Circular	Mumbai
2	1987	20 Rupees	25 Gms	Cupro Nickel	39 Mm	Milled, Serr.180	Circular	Mumbai
3	1987	1rupees	6 Gms	Cupro Nickel	26 Mm	Milled, Serr.204	Circular	Mumbai

JAWAHARLALA NEHRU BIRTH CENTENARY (1989)

Date of Issue:14th NOVEMBER 1988

OBVERSE DESCRIPTION OF COIN
Asoka lion capital, denomination below, Bharat/India on sides

REVERSE DESCRIPTION OF COIN
Bust-Jawarlal Nehru, Date below-1989, legend-Jawaharlal Nehru Centenary.

Sl No	Year	Denomi-nation	Weight of the Coin	Metal Com-positions	Shape & Size			Mint
					Dia	Edge	Shape	
1	1989	100 Rupees	35 Gms	Quaternary Allloy	44 Mm	Milled, Serr.200	Circular	Mumbai
2	1989	20 Rupees	25 Gms	Cupro Nickel	39 Mm	Milled, Serr.180	Circular	Mumbai
3	1985	5 Rupees	12.5 Gms	Cupro Nickel	31 Mm	Milled, Serr. 150	Circular	Mumbai
4	1989	1 Rupees	6 Gms	Cupro Nickel	26 Mm	Milled, Serr.204	Circular	Mumbai

DR. B.R. AMBEDKAR
(1990)

Date of Issue: 1990

OBVERSE DESCRIPTION OF COIN

Asoka lion capital, denomination below, Bharat/India on sides

REVERSE DESCRIPTION OF COIN

Bust of DR. B.R. AMBEDKAR, Date 1990, Legend "Dr. B.R. Ambedkar CENTENARY

Sl No	Year	Denom-ination	Weight of the Coin	Metal Compo-sitions	Shape & Size			Mint
					Dia	Edge	Shape	
1	1990	1 Rupee	6 Gms	Cupro-Nickel	26 Mm	Milled,, Serr.204	Circular	Mumbai

WORLD FOOD DAY – FOOD FOR FUTURE (1990)

Date of Issue: 1990

OBVERSE DESCRIPTION OF COIN

Asoka lion capital, denomination below, Bharat/India on sides

REVERSE DESCRIPTION OF COIN

Agricultural Family, Date below 1990, Legend food for the future, 16 October 1990, World Food day"

Sl No	Year	Denom-ination	Weight of the Coin	Metal Compo-sitions	Shape & Size			Mint
					Dia	Edge	Shape	
1	1990	1 Rupee	6 Gms	Cupro-Nickel	26 Mm	Milled,, Serr.204	Circular	Mumbai

37th COMMONWEALTH PARLIAMENTARY CONFERENCE

Date of Issue: 23rd SEPTEMBER 1991

OBVERSE DESCRIPTION OF COIN

Ashoka Lion Capital, denomination below, Bharat/India on sides.

REVERSE DESCRIPTION OF COIN

Indian Parliamentary Building with flag, Date above-1991,Legend ' common wealth parliamentary conference"

Sl No	Year	Denomi-nation	Weight of the Coin	Metal Compo-sitions	Shape & Size			Mint
					Dia	Edge	Shape	
1	1991	10 Rupees	25 Gms	Cupro Nickel	39 Mm	Milled, Serr.180	Circular	Mumbai
2	1991	5 Rupees	12.5 Gms	Cupro Nickel	31 Mm	Milled, Serr. 150	Circular	Mumbai
3	1991	1 Rupees	6 Gms	Cupro Nickel	26 Mm	Milled, Serr.204	Circular	Mumbai

INDIAN TOURISM YEAR
(1991)

Date of Issue: 25th DECEMBER 1991

OBVERSE DESCRIPTION OF COIN

Ashoka Lion Capital, denomination below, Bharat/India on sides.

REVERSE DESCRIPTION OF COIN

STYLIZED PEACOCK DANCING, DATE BELOW-1991, LEGEND: "TOURISM YEAR"

Sl No	Year	Denomi-nation	Weight of the Coin	Metal Composi-tions	Shape & Size			Mint
					Dia	Edge	Shape	
1	1991	5 Rupees	12.5 Gms	Cupro Nickel	31 Mm	Milled, Serr.150	Circular	Mumbai
2	1991	2 Rupees	8 Gms	Cupro Nickel	28 Mm	Milled, S.e Serr. 200	Circular	Mumbai
3	1991	1 Rupees	6 Gms	Cupro Nickel	26 Mm	Milled, Serr.204	Circular	Mumbai

RAJIV GANDHI
(1944-1991)

Date of Issue: 25th DECEMBER 1992

OBVERSE DESCRIPTION OF COIN

Ashoka Lion Capital, denomination below, Bharat/India on sides.

REVERSE DESCRIPTION OF COIN

Bust of Rajiv Gandhi, Date Below 1944-1991, Legend-Rajib Gandhi

SI No	Year	Denomi-nation	Weight of the Coin	Metal Com-positions	Shape & Size			Mint
					Dia	Edge	Shape	
1	1992	1 Rupee	6 Gms	Cupro Nickel	26 Mm	Milled, Serr.204	Circular	Mumbai

QUIT INDIA MOVEMENT (1992)

Date of Issue: 1992

OBVERSE DESCRIPTION OF COIN

Ashoka Lion Capital, denomination below, Bharat/India on sides

REVERSE DESCRIPTION OF COIN

Quit Indian Movement Monument, date below-1942-1992, legend "Quit india movement Golden jubilee"

SI No	Year	Denomi-nation	Weight of the Coin	Metal Com-positions	Shape & Size			Mint
					Dia	Edge	Shape	
1	1992	100 Rupees	35 Gms	Cupro Nickel	44 Mm	Milled, Serr.200	Circular	Mumbai
2	1992	50 Rupees	30 Gms	Cupro Nickel	39 Mm	Milled, Serr.180	Circular	Mumbai
3	1992	10 Rupees	9 Gms	Cupro Nickel	31 Mm	Milled, Serr. 150	Circular	Mumbai
4	1992	1 Rupees	6 Gms	Cupro Nickel	26 Mm	Milled, Serr.204	Circular	Mumbai

LAND VITAL RESOURSE
(1992)

Date of Issue: 18th November 1993

OBVERSE DESCRIPTION OF COIN

Ashoka Lion Capital, denomination below, Bharat/India on sides

REVERSE DESCRIPTION OF COIN

Tree with weavy lines representing land, date below-1992, legend, Land Vital resource, National land Vital resource, National land conservation week 14-20 nov-1992"

SI No	Year	Denomination	Weight of the Coin	Metal Compositions	Shape & Size			Mint
					Dia	Edge	Shape	
1	1992	2 Rupees	6	Cupro Nickel	26	Hendecagonal (11 Sided)	Plain	Calcutta

WORLD FOOD DAY AND NUTRITION (1992)

Date of Issue: 18th November 1993

OBVERSE DESCRIPTION OF COIN

Ashoka Lion Capital, denomination below, Bharat/India on sides

REVERSE DESCRIPTION OF COIN

FAO symbol, food item left of grain stalks legend "Food and Nutrition"and "world food day" with year 1992"

Sl No	Year	Denom-ination	Weight of the Coin	Metal Com-positions	Shape & Size			Mint
					Dia	Edge	Shape	
1	1992	1 Rupee	6 Gms	Cupro Nickel	26 Mm	Milled, Serr.204	Circular	Mumbai

89th INTER PARLIMENTARY UNION CONFERENCE

Date of Issue: 11th APRIL 1993

OBVERSE DESCRIPTION OF COIN
Ashoka Lion Capital, denomination below, Bharat/India on sides

REVERSE DESCRIPTION OF COIN
Indian Parliamentary Building with flag, date above-1993, Legend "89th inter Parliamentary union Conference"

Sl No	Year	Denom- ination	Weight of the Coin	Metal Com- positions	Shape & Size			Mint
					Dia	Edge	Shape	
1	1993	10 Rupees	25 Gms	Cupro Nickel	39 Mm	Milled, Serr. 180	Circular	Mumbai
2	1993	5 Rupees	12.5 Gms	Cupro Nickel	31 Mm	Milled, Serr.150	Circular	Mumbai
3	1993	1 Rupees	6 Gms	Cupro Nickel	26 Mm	Milled, Serr.204	Circular	Mumbai

75th ANNIVERSARY OF INTERNATIONAL LABOUR ORGANIZATION

Date of Issue: 27th OCTOBER 1994

OBVERSE DESCRIPTION OF COIN

Ashoka Lion Capital, denomination below, Bharat/India on sides

REVERSE DESCRIPTION OF COIN

ILO inside the circle of wreaths Date below-1919-1994-Legend "world of work"

Sl No	Year	Denomina-tion	Weight of the Coin	Metal Com-positions	Shape & Size			Mint
					Dia	Edge	Shape	
1	1994	100 Rupees	35 Gms	Quaternary Allloy	44 Mm	Milled, Serr.200	Circular	Mumbai
2	1994	50 Rupees	30 Gms	Cupro Nickel	39 Mm	Milled, Serr.180	Circular	Mumbai
3	1994	5 Rupees	9 Gms	Cupro Nickel	23 Mm	Milled, S.e, Serr. 100	Circular	Mumbai

WORLD FOOD DAY – WATER FOR LIFE

Date of Issue: 27th OCTOBER 1994

OBVERSE DESCRIPTION OF COIN

Ashoka Lion Capital, denomination below, Bharat/India on sides

REVERSE DESCRIPTION OF COIN

Water Drop, Logo of FAO, date Below: 1994, Legend "water for life: world Food day.

Sl No	Year	Denomi-nation	Weight of the Coin	Metal Com-positions	Shape & Size			Mint
					Dia	Edge	Shape	
1	1994	2 Rupees	6 Gms	Cupro-Nickel	26 Mm	Milled, Serr.200	Circular	Kolkata

INTERNATIONAL YEAR OF THE FAMILY (1994)

Date of Issue: 1994

OBVERSE DESCRIPTION OF COIN
Ashoka Lion Capital, denomination below, Bharat/India on sides

REVERSE DESCRIPTION OF COIN
Water Drop, Logo of FAO, date Below: 1994, Legend "water for life: world Food day.

SI No	Year	Denomi-nation	Weight of the Coin	Metal Com-positions	Shape & Size			Mint
					Dia	Edge	Shape	
1	1995	1 Rupees	35 Gms	Quaternary Allloy	44 Mm	Milled, Serr.200	Circular	Mumbai

GLOBALIZING INDIAN AGRICULTURE: AGRI EXPO 95

Date of Issue: 27th OCTOBER 1994

OBVERSE DESCRIPTION OF COIN

Ashoka Lion Capital, denomination below, Bharat/India on sides

REVERSE DESCRIPTION OF COIN

CATTLE HEAD WITH A PLOUGH AND HOEON EITHER SIDE, Legend "Globalizing Indian Agriculture Agri Expo 95"

SI No	Year	Denomi-nation	Weight of the Coin	Metal Compo-sitions	Shape & Size			Mint
					Dia	Edge	Shape	
1	1995	2 Rupees	6 Gms	Cupro-Nickel	26 Mm	Milled, Serr.200	Circular	Kolkata

8th WORLD TAMIL CONFERENCE (SAINT THIRUVALLUVAR)

Date of Issue: 1995

OBVERSE DESCRIPTION OF COIN

Ashoka Lion Capital, denomination below, Bharat/India on sides

REVERSE DESCRIPTION OF COIN

Seated saint facing right, legend ' 8th world Tamil conference: Saint Thiruvallur.

Sl No	Year	Denomi-nation	Weight of the Coin	Metal Com-positions	Shape & Size			Mint
					Dia	Edge	Shape	
1	1995	1 Rupees	35 Gms	Quaternary Allloy	44 Mm	Milled, Serr.200	Circular	Mumbai
2	1995	2 Rupees	35 Gms	Quaternary Allloy	44 Mm	Milled, Serr.200	Circular	Mumbai
3	1995	5 Rupees	35 Gms	Quaternary Allloy	44 Mm	Milled, Serr.200	Circular	Mumbai

2nd INTERNATIONAL CROP SCIENCE CONGRES (1996)

Date of Issue: 17 to 24th NOVEMBER 1996

OBVERSE DESCRIPTION OF COIN

Ashoka Lion Capital, denomination below, Bharat/India on sides

REVERSE DESCRIPTION OF COIN

Plants on Glove Spray below, Brade above, Date below-1996, Legend –"International Crop science Congress"

Sl No	Year	Denomination	Weight of the Coin	Metal Compositions	Shape & Size			Mint
					Dia	Edge	Shape	
1	1996	5 Rupees	9 Gms	Cupro Nickel	23 Mm	Security Edge /100	Circular	Calcutta

NETAJI SUBHAS CHANDRA BOSE (1996)

Date of Issue: 1997

OBVERSE DESCRIPTION OF COIN

Ashoka Lion Capital, denomination below, Bharat/India on sides

REVERSE DESCRIPTION OF COIN

Bust of Netaji Subhas Chandra Bose, Date of Below-1996 *Legend, Subash Chandra Bose centenary.*

Sl No	Year	Denomi-nation	Weight of the Coin	Metal Composi-tions	Shape & Size			Mint
					Dia	Edge	Shape	
1	1996	2 Rupees	6	Cupro Nickel	26	Hendecagonal (11 Sided)	Circular	Calcutta

SARDAR VALLABH BHAI PATEL (1996)

Date of Issue: 1996

OBVERSE DESCRIPTION OF COIN

Ashoka Lion Capital, denomination below, Bharat/India on sides

REVERSE DESCRIPTION OF COIN

BUST OF SARDAR VALLBHBHAI PATEL DATE BELOW 1996, LEGEND "SARDAR VALLABHBHAI PATEL"

Sl No	Year	Denomi- nation	Weight of the Coin	Metal Com- positions	Shape & Size			Mint
					Dia	Edge	Shape	
1	1996	100 Rupees	35 Gms	Quaternary Allloy	44 Mm	Milled, Serr.200	Circular	Mumbai
2	1996	50 Rupees	30 Gms	Cupro Nickel	39 Mm	Milled, Serr.180	Circular	Mumbai
3	1996	10 Rupees	12.50 Gms	Cupro Nickel	31 Mm	Milled, S.e, Serr. 150	Circular	Mumbai
4	1996	2 Rupees	6 Gms	Cupro Nickel	26 Mm	Flat To Corner	11 Sided	Mumbai

NETAJI SUBHAS CHANDRA BOSE (1997)

Date of Issue: 1997

OBVERSE DESCRIPTION OF COIN

Ashoka Lion Capital, denomination below, Bharat/India on sides

REVERSE DESCRIPTION OF COIN

Bust of Subhas Chandra Bose, Date Below-1997, Legend Netaji Subhas Chandra Bose Centenary.

Sl No	Year	Denomi-nation	Weight of the Coin	Metal Com-positions	Shape & Size			Mint
					Dia	Edge	Shape	
1	1997	100 Rupees	35	S50	44	Milled /200	Circular	Kolkata
2	1997	50 Rupees	30	Cupro Nickel	39	Milled /180	Circular	Kolkata
3	1997	10 Rupees	12.5	Cupro Nickel	31	Milled /150	Circular	Kolkata
4	1997	2 Rupees	6	Cupro Nickel	26	Plain	Hendecagonal (11 Sided)	Kolkata

IPU – MEN AND WOMEN PARTNERSHIP IN POLITICS

Date of Issue: 1997

OBVERSE DESCRIPTION OF COIN

Ashoka Lion Capital, denomination below, Bharat/India on sides

REVERSE DESCRIPTION OF COIN

Parilament House with national Flag and Logo, Date Below-1997, Legend Inter parliament Conference at top 'Men & Women in Partnership in politics" at below.

Sl No	Year	Denomina-tion	Weight of the Coin	Metal Com-positions	Shape & Size			Mint
					Dia	Edge	Shape	
1	1997	50 Rupees	35	Cupro Nickel	44	Milled /180	Circular	Kolkata
2	1997	10 Rupees	30	Cupro Nickel	39	Milled /150	Circular	Kolkata
3	1997	5 Rupees	9	Cupro Nickel	23	Plain	Hendecagonal (11 Sided)	Kolkata

50ᵗʰ ANNIVERSARY OF INDEPENDENCE

Date of Issue: 30ᵗʰ December 1997

OBVERSE DESCRIPTION OF COIN

Ashoka Lion Capital, denomination below, Bharat/India on sides

REVERSE DESCRIPTION OF COIN

Mahatma Gandhi Marching with followers Date below-1947-1997 Legend-50ᵗʰ year independence

Sl No	Year	Denomi-nation	Weight of the Coin	Metal Composi-tions	Shape & Size			Mint
					Dia	Edge	Shape	
1	1997	50 Rupees	30	Quatyerny Allow	39	Plain	Circular	Mumbai
2	1997	50 Paisa	3.79	Ferattic Stainless Steel	22	Plain	Circular	Mumbai

CELLULAR JAIL

Date of Issue: 30th December 1997

Ashoka Lion Capital, denomination below, Bharat/India on sides

OBVERSE DESCRIPTION OF COIN

Cellular jail in Port Blair, Date Below 1997, legend" Cellular Jail Port Blair"

SI No	Year	Denomina-tion	Weight of the Coin	Metal Composi-tions	Shape & Size			Mint
					Dia	Edge	Shape	
1	1997	1 Rupees	4.85	Ss	25	Plain	Circular	Calcutta

SRI AUROBINDO ALL LIFE IS YOGA (1998)

Date of Issue: 24th NOVEMBER 1998

OBVERSE DESCRIPTION OF COIN

Ashoka Lion Capital, denomination below, Bharat/India on sides

REVERSE DESCRIPTION OF COIN

Bust of Sri Aurobindo, Date below-1998, Legend "Sri Aurobindo" All life of Yoga.

Sl No	Year	Denomina-tion	Weight of the Coin	Metal Com-positions	Shape & Size			Mint
					Dia	Edge	Shape	
1	1998	100 Rupees	35 Gms	Quaternary Allloy	44 Mm	Milled, Serr.200	Circular	Mumbai
2	1998	50 Rupees	30 Gms	Cupro Nickel	39 Mm	Milled, Serr.180	Circular	Mumbai
3	1998	10 Rupees	12.50 Gms	Cupro Nickel	31 Mm	Milled, Serr. 150	Circular	Mumbai
4	1998	2 Rupees	6 Gms	Cupro Nickel	26 Mm	Flat To Corner	11 Sided	Mumbai

DESHBANDHU CHITTARANJAN DAS (1870-1925)

Date of Issue: 27th December 1998

OBVERSE DESCRIPTION OF COIN
Ashoka Lion Capital, denomination below, Bharat/India on sides

REVERSE DESCRIPTION OF COIN
Bust of Deshbandhu chittaranjan Das, Date below-1998, Legend – Deshbandhu Chittaranjan Das 1870-1925.

Sl No	Year	Denomina-tion	Weight of the Coin	Metal Com-positions	Shape & Size			Mint
					Dia	Edge	Shape	
1	1998	100 Rupees	35	S50	44	Milled /200	Circular	Kolkata
2	1998	50 Rupees	30	Cupro Nickel	39	Milled /180	Circular	Kolkata
3	1998	10 Rupees	12.5	Cupro Nickel	31	Milled /150	Circular	Kolkata
4	1998	2 Rupees	6	Cupro Nickel	26	Plain	Hendecagonal (11 Sided)	Kolkata

₹

CHHATRAPATI SHIVAJI
(1999)

Date of Issue:1999

OBVERSE DESCRIPTION OF COIN
Ashoka Lion Capital, denomination below, Bharat/India on sides

REVERSE DESCRIPTION OF COIN
Bust of Chatrapati Shivaji, Date-1999, Legend –Chhatrapati Shivajie

Sl No	Year	Denomina-tion	Weight of the Coin	Metal Com-positions	Shape & Size			Mint
					Dia	Edge	Shape	
1	1999	100 Rupees	35 Gms	Quaternary Allloy	44 Mm	Milled, Serr.200	Circular	Mumbai
2	1999	50 Rupees	30 Gms	Cupro Nickel	39 Mm	Milled, Serr.180	Circular	Mumbai
3	1999	2 Rupees	6 Gms	Cupro Nickel	26 Mm	Flat To Corner	11 Sided	Mumbai

SAINT DHYANESWAR
(AD1274-1926)

Date of Issue: 1999

OBVERSE DESCRIPTION OF COIN
Ashoka Lion Capital, denomination below, Bharat/India on sides

REVERSE DESCRIPTION OF COIN
Figure of Saint Dnyaneshwar Date-1999, Legend "Saint Dnyaneshwar"

Sl No	Year	Denomi-nation	Weight of the Coin	Metal Compo-sitions	Shape & Size			Mint
					Dia	Edge	Shape	
1	100 Rupee	22.50 Gms	Quaternary Allloy	39 Mm	Milled, Serr.180	Circular	Mumbai	100 Rupee
2	1 Rupees	6 Gms	Cupro Nickel	26 Mm	Flat To Corner	11 Sided	Mumbai	1 Rupees

GOLDEN JUBILEE CELEBRATION OF SUPREME COURT (1950-2000)

Date of Issue: 26th JUNE 1999

OBVERSE DESCRIPTION OF COIN
Ashoka Lion Capital, denomination below, Bharat/India on sides

REVERSE DESCRIPTION OF COIN
Motif of Supreme Court of India, Date Below: 1950-2000, Legend – Supreme Court of India.

Sl No	Year	Denomi-nation	Weight of the Coin	Metal Com-positions	Shape & Size			Mint
					Dia	Edge	Shape	
1	2000	50 Rupee	22.50 Gms	Quaternary Allloy	39 Mm	Milled, Serr.180	Circular	Mumbai
2	2000	2 Rupees	6 Gms	Cupro Nickel	26 Mm	Flat To Corner	11 Sided	Mumbai

DR. SYAMA PRASAD MOOKERJEE CENTENARY (2002)

Date of Issue: 05th APRIL 2002

OBVERSE DESCRIPTION OF COIN

Ashoka Lion Capital, denomination below, Bharat/India on sides

REVERSE DESCRIPTION OF COIN

Bust of Dr. Syama Prasad Mookerjee, Date; 2001 below, Legend" Dr Syama Prasad Mookerjee Centenary 2001"

Sl No	Year	Denomination	Weight of the Coin	Metal Compositions	Shape & Size			Mint
					Dia	Edge	Shape	
1	2002	100 Rupees	35	S50	44	Milled /200	Circular	Kolkata
2	2002	50 Rupees	30	Cupro Nickel	39	Milled /180	Circular	Kolkata
3	2002	10 Rupees	12.5	Cupro Nickel	31	Milled /150	Circular	Kolkata
4	2002	2 Rupees	6	Cupro Nickel	26	Plain	Hendecagonal (11 Sided)	Kolkata

BHAGAWAN MAHAVIR – 2600th JANM KALYANAK

Date of Issue: 2001

OBVERSE DESCRIPTION OF COIN

Ashoka Lion Capital, denomination below, Bharat/India on sides

REVERSE DESCRIPTION OF COIN

Jain Symbol, Date-2001 Below, Legend – Bhagwan mahavir 2600th Janm Kalyank"

SI No	Year	Denomi-nation	Weight of the Coin	Metal Com-positions	Shape & Size			Mint
					Dia	Edge	Shape	
1	2001	10 Rupees	35 Gms	Quanternary Alloy	44 Mm	Milled	Circular	Mumbai
2	2001	5 Rupees	9 Gms	Cupro-Nickel	23 Mm	Milled	Circular	Mumbai

LOKNAYAK JAYA PRAKASH NARAYAN

Date of Issue: 11th OCTOBER 2002

OBVERSE DESCRIPTION OF COIN

Ashoka Lion Capital, denomination below, Bharat/India on sides

REVERSE DESCRIPTION OF COIN

Bust of Loknayak jaya prakash Narayan, Date: 2002 Below, Legend"
lokanayak "Jaya Prakash Narayan Cenetary"

Sl No	Year	Denomina-tion	Weight of the Coin	Metal Com-positions	Shape & Size			Mint
					Dia	Edge	Shape	
1	2002	100 Rupees	35 Gms	Quaternary Allloy	44 Mm	Milled, Serr.200	Circular	Mumbai
2	2002	10 Rupees	12.5 Gms	Cupro Nickel	31 Mm	Milled, Serr.150	Circular	Mumbai
3	2002	1 Rupee	4.85 Gms	Ferritic Stainless Steel	25 Mm	Unmilled	Circular	Mumbai

SANT TUKARAM

Date of Issue: 2002

OBVERSE DESCRIPTION OF COIN
Ashoka Lion Capital, denomination below, Bharat/India on sides

REVERSE DESCRIPTION OF COIN
Sant Tukaram seated figure, Date: 2002 Below, Legend" Sant Tukaram"

Sl No	Year	Denomination	Weight of the Coin	Metal Compositions	Shape & Size			Mint
					Dia	Edge	Shape	
1	2002	100 Rupees	35 Gms	Quaternary Allloy	44 Mm	Milled, Serr.200	Circular	Kolkata
2	2002	50 Rupees	30 Gms	Cupro Nickel	39 Mm	Milled	Circular	Kolkata
3	2002	10 Rupees	12.5 Gms	Cupro Nickel	31 Mm	Milled, Serr.150	Circular	Kolkata
4	2002	1 Rupee	4.85 Gms	Cupro Nickel	25 Mm	Unmilled	Circular	Kolkata

150 GLORIOUS YEARS OF RAILWAYS

Date of Issue: 2003

OBVERSE DESCRIPTION OF COIN

Ashoka Lion Capital, denomination below, Bharat/India on sides

REVERSE DESCRIPTION OF COIN

Elephant, The guard showing the lantem, Date-2003 Below, Legend-Glowrious 150 years of Railways.

Sl No	Year	Denomina-tion	Weight of the Coin	Metal Com-positions	Shape & Size			Mint
					Dia	Edge	Shape	
1	2003	100 Rupees	35 Gms	Quaternary Allloy	44 Mm	Milled, Serr.200	Circular	Kolkata
2	2003	2 Rupees	6 Gms	Cupro Nickel	26 Mm	Milled	Hende-cagonal	Kolkata

VEER DURGADAS RATHOD

Date of Issue: 26th AUGUST 2003

OBVERSE DESCRIPTION OF COIN

Ashoka Lion Capital, denomination below, Bharat/India on sides

REVERSE DESCRIPTION OF COIN

Bust of veer Durga dass Rathore, Date-2003 below, Legend-Veer Durga Dass Rathore.

Sl No	Year	Denomina-tion	Weight of the Coin	Metal Com-positions	Shape & Size			Mint
					Dia	Edge	Shape	
1	2003	100 Rupees	35 Gms	Quaternary Allloy	44 Mm	Milled, Serr.200	Circular	Mumbai
2	2003	10 Rupees	12.5 Gms	Cupro Nickel	31 Mm	Milled, Serr.150	Circular	Mumbai
3	2003	1 Rupee	4.85 Gms	Ferritic Stainless Steel	25 Mm	Un-milled	Circular	Mumbai

MAHARANA PRATAP

Date of Issue: 04th JUNE 2003

OBVERSE DESCRIPTION OF COIN
Ashoka Lion Capital, denomination below, Bharat/India on sides

REVERSE DESCRIPTION OF COIN
Bust of Maharana Pratap, Date-2003 below, legend Maharana Pratap "1540-1597"

SI No	Year	Denomination	Weight of the Coin	Metal Compositions	Shape & Size			Mint
					Dia	Edge	Shape	
1	2003	100 Rupees	35 Gms	Quaternary Allloy	44 Mm	Milled, Serr.200	Circular	Mumbai
2	2003	10 Rupees	12.5 Gms	Cupro Nickel	31 Mm	Milled, Serr.150	Circular	Mumbai
3	2003	1 Rupee	4.85 Gms	Ferritic Stainless Steel	25 Mm	Unmilled	Circular	Mumbai

DADA BHAI NAOROJI
(1825-1917)

Date of Issue: 2003

OBVERSE DESCRIPTION OF COIN

Ashoka Lion Capital, denomination below, Bharat/India on sides

REVERSE DESCRIPTION OF COIN

Bust of Dada Bhai Naoroji, Date: 1825-1917 Below, L`egend "Dada Bhai Naoroji"

Sl No	Year	Denomination	Weight of the Coin	Metal Compositions	Shape & Size			Mint
					Dia	Edge	Shape	
1	2003	5 Rupees	9 Gms	Cupro Nickel	23 Mm	Milled, S.e, Serr.100	Circular	Mumbai

150 YEARS OF TELECOMMUNICATIONS (2005)

Date of Issue: 2005

OBVERSE DESCRIPTION OF COIN

Ashoka Lion Capital, denomination below, Bharat/India on sides

REVERSE DESCRIPTION OF COIN

Pigeon carrying a mobile phone, Date-2004 Below, Legend" 150 Years of Telecommunication"

Sl No	Year	Denomina-tion	Weight of the Coin	Metal Com-positions	Shape & Size			Mint
					Dia	Edge	Shape	
1	2004	100 Rupees	35 Gms	Quaternary Alloy	44 Mm	Milled	Circuolar	Kolkata
2	2004	2 Rupees	6 Gms	Cupro Nickel	26 Mm	Milled	Hende-cagonal	Kolkata

150 YEARS OF INDIA POST (2004)

Date of Issue: 2004

OBVERSE DESCRIPTION OF COIN
Ashoka Lion Capital, denomination below, Bharat/India on sides

REVERSE DESCRIPTION OF COIN
150 years at center with india Post logo, Date: 2004 below, Legend – "India Post"

SI No	Year	Denomi-nation	Weight of the Coin	Metal Compo-sitions	Shape & Size			Mint
					Dia	Edge	Shape	
1	2004	100 Rupees	35 Gms	Quaterneely Allow	44 Mm	Milled	Circular	Kolkata
2	2004	1 Rupees	4.85 Gms	Ferratic Stain-less Steel	25 Mm	Milled	Circular	Kolkata

SHRI K. KAMRAJ CENTENARY

Date of Issue: 27th OCTOBER 2004

OBVERSE DESCRIPTION OF COIN

Ashoka Lion Capital, denomination below, Bharat/India on sides

REVERSE DESCRIPTION OF COIN

BUST OF K. KAMRAJ, Date-1903-1975 Below, Legend "K Kamraj"

Sl No	Year	Denomina-tion	Weight of the Coin	Metal Com-positions	Shape & Size			Mint
					Dia	Edge	Shape	
1	2004	100 Rupees	35 Gms	Quaternely Alloy	44 Mm	Milled, S.e, Serr.100	Circular	Mumbai
2	2004	5 Rupees	9 Gms	Cupro Nickel	23 Mm	Milled, S.e, Serr.100	Circular	Mumbai

LALBAHADUR SHASTRI BIRTH CENTENARY (1904-2004)

Date of Issue: 04ᵗʰ October 2005

OBVERSE DESCRIPTION OF COIN

Ashoka Lion Capital, denomination below, Bharat/India on sides

REVERSE DESCRIPTION OF COIN

Bust of Lal Bahadur shastri, Date-1904-2004 below, Legend "lal bahadur Shastri Birth Centenary"

SI No	Year	Denomina-tion	Weight of the Coin	Metal Composi-tions	Shape & Size			Mint
					Dia	Edge	Shape	
1	2004	100 Rupees	35 Gms	S50	44 Mm	Milled /200	Circular	Kolkata
2	2004	5 Rupees	9 Gms	Cupro Nickel	23 Mm	Security Edge /100	Circular	Kolkata

UNITY IN DIVERSITY

Date of Issue:2004

OBVERSE DESCRIPTION OF COIN

Ashoka Lion Capital, denomination below, Bharat/India on sides

REVERSE DESCRIPTION OF COIN

Double plus symbol with 4 dots to represent, 4 heads joined by common body, denomination above.

Type I: Unity in Diversity

SI No	Year	Denomina-tion	Weight of the Coin	Metal Com-positions	Shape & Size			Mint
					Dia	Edge	Shape	
1	2005	100 Rupees	7.71 Gms	Bi-Mettalic	27 Mm	Milled, Serr.200	Circular	Kolkata
2	2005	5 Rupees	6 Gms	Ferratic Stainless Steel	23 Mm	Milled, S.e, Serr.100	Circular	Kolkata
3	2005	2 Rupees	5.8 Gms	Ferratic Stainless Steel	27 Mm	Milled	Circular	Kolkata
4	2005	1 Rupee	4.95 Gms	Ferratic Stainless Steel	25 Mm	Milled	Circular	Kolkata

75th YEARS OF DANDI MARCH

Date of Issue:02nd OCTOBER 2005

OBVERSE DESCRIPTION OF COIN
Ashoka Lion Capital, denomination below, Bharat/India on sides

REVERSE DESCRIPTION OF COIN
Mahtma Gandhi with followers marching Dandi, Date-1930-2005 Below, Legend '75 Years of Dandi March"

SI No	Year	Denomi-nation	Weight of the Coin	Metal Com-positions	Shape & Size			Mint
					Dia	Edge	Shape	
1	2005	100 Ru-pees	35 Gms	Quaternary Allloy	44 Mm	Milled, Serr.200	Circular	Kolkata
2	2005	5 Rupees	9 Gms	Cupro Nickel	23 Mm	Milled, S.e, Serr.100	Circular	Kolkata

JAGAT GURU SREE NARAYANA GURUDEV

Date of Issue: 07th SEPTEMBER 2006

OBVERSE DESCRIPTION OF COIN

Ashoka Lion Capital, denomination below, Bharat/India on sides

REVERSE DESCRIPTION OF COIN

Bust of Narayana Gurudev, No Date Mentioned, Legend "Jagath guru shree naryan Gurudev"

Sl No	Year	Denomination	Weight of the Coin	Metal Compositions	Shape & Size			Mint
					Dia	Edge	Shape	
1	2006	100 Rupees	35 Gms	Quaternary Allloy	44 Mm	Milled, Serr.200	Circular	Mumbai
2	2006	5 Rupees	9 Gms	Cupro Nickel	23 Mm	Milled, S.e, Serr.100	Circular	Mumbai

MAHATMA BASAVESHWARA

Date of Issue: 2006

OBVERSE DESCRIPTION OF COIN
Ashoka Lion Capital, denomination below, Bharat/India on sides

REVERSE DESCRIPTION OF COIN
Bust of Mahatma Basveshwara, No Date Mentioned, Legend "Mahatma Basaveshwara"

SI No	Year	Denomi-nation	Weight of the Coin	Metal Com-positions	Shape & Size			Mint
					Dia	Edge	Shape	
1	2006	100 Rupees	35 Gms	Quaternary Allloy	44 Mm	Milled, Serr.200	Circular	Mumbai
2	2006	5 Rupees	9 Gms	Cupro Nickel	23 Mm	Milled, S.e, Serr.100	Circular	Mumbai

200 YEARS OF STATE BANK OF INDIA

Date of Issue: 2006

OBVERSE DESCRIPTION OF COIN
Ashoka Lion Capital, denomination below, Bharat/India on sides

REVERSE DESCRIPTION OF COIN
Logo of state bank of India, Date 2006, below, Legend" state bank of India"

SI No	Year	Denomina-tion	Weight of the Coin	Metal Com-positions	Shape & Size			Mint
					Dia	Edge	Shape	
1	2006	100 Rupees	35 Gms	Quaternary Allloy	44 Mm	Milled, Serr.200	Circular	Mumbai
2	2006	5 Rupees	9 Gms	Cupro Nickel	23 Mm	Milled, S.e, Serr.100	Circular	Mumbai

50 YEAR GOLDEN JUBILEE OF ONGC (1956-2006)

Date of Issue: 2006

OBVERSE DESCRIPTION OF COIN

Ashoka Lion Capital, denomination below, Bharat/India on sides

REVERSE DESCRIPTION OF COIN

ONGC Above, logo inside 0 of numeral 50, Date:1956-2006 Below," celebrating India"

Sl No	Year	Denomi-nation	Weight of the Coin	Metal Compo-sitions	Shape & Size			Mint
					Dia	Edge	Shape	
1	2006	50 Rupees	35 Gms	Quaternary Allloy	44 Mm	Milled, Serr.200	Circular	Mumbai
2	2006	5 Rupees	9 Gms	Cupro Nickel	23 Mm	Milled, S.e, Serr.100	Circular	Mumbai

105th BIRTH ANNIVERSARY OF LOKAMANYA BAL GANGADHAR TILAK

Date of Issue:23rd JULY 2007

OBVERSE DESCRIPTION OF COIN

Ashoka Lion Capital, denomination below, Bharat/India on sides

REVERSE DESCRIPTION OF COIN

Bust of Bal gangadhar Tilak, Date 2007 Below, Legend"150th Birth Anniversary of Lokmanya bal gangadhar tilak

Sl No	Year	Denomi-nation	Weight of the Coin	Metal Com-positions	Shape & Size			Mint
					Dia	Edge	Shape	
1	2007	100 Rupees	35 Gms	Quaternary Allloy	44 Mm	Milled, Serr.200	Circular	Mumbai
2	2007	5 Rupees	9 Gms	Cupro Nickel	23 Mm	Milled, S.e, Serr.100	Circular	Mumbai

150 YEARS OF FIRST WAR OF INDEPENDENCE

Date of Issue: 18th APRIL 2007

OBVERSE DESCRIPTION OF COIN

Ashoka Lion Capital, denomination below, Bharat/India on sides

REVERSE DESCRIPTION OF COIN

Portraits of Freedom fighters. Date-1958-2007 Below, Legend: The First war of independence, 150 years.

SI No	Year	Denomi- nation	Weight of the Coin	Metal Com- positions	Shape & Size			Mint
					Dia	Edge	Shape	
1	2007	100 Ru- pees	35 Gms	Quaternary Allloy	44 Mm	Milled, Serr.200	Circular	Mumbai
2	2007	5 Rupees	9 Gms	Cupro Nickel	23 Mm	Milled, S.e, Serr.100	Circular	Mumbai

PLATINUM JUBILEE CELEBRATION OF INDIA AIR FORCE (1932-2007)

Date of Issue: 2006

OBVERSE DESCRIPTION OF COIN

Ashoka Lion Capital, denomination below, Bharat/India on sides

REVERSE DESCRIPTION OF COIN

First Fighter Air craft 'Wapiti and combat SU-30 MK 1 at center, Date 1932-2007 Below, legend "Platinum Jubilee of Indian Air force"

Sl No	Year	Denomination	Weight of the Coin	Metal Compositions	Shape & Size			Mint
					Dia	Edge	Shape	
1	2006	50 Rupees	35 Gms	Quaternary Allloy	44 Mm	Milled, Serr.200	Circular	Mumbai
2	2006	2 Rupees	5.62 Gms	Ferratic Stainless Steel	27 Mm	Milled, S.e, Serr.100	Circular	Mumbai

GOLDEN JUBILEE CELEBRATION OF KHADI & VILLAGE INDUSTRIES COMMISSION 50 YEARS

Date of Issue: 19th NOVEMBER 2007

OBVERSE DESCRIPTION OF COIN

Ashoka Lion Capital, denomination below, Bharat/India on sides

REVERSE DESCRIPTION OF COIN

Bust of Mahatma Gandhi with Charaka and village scene, legend 50 Years of Khadi & village industries commission.

SI No	Year	Denomi-nation	Weight of the Coin	Metal Com-positions	Shape & Size			Mint
					Dia	Edge	Shape	
1	2007	50 Rupees	22.5 Gms	Quaternary Allloy	44 Mm	Milled, Serr.200	Circular	Mumbai
2	2007	5 Rupees	9 Gms	Cupro Nickel	23 Mm	Milled, S.e, Serr.100	Circular	Mumbai

SHAHEED BHAGAT SINGH BIRTH CENTENARY (1907-2008)

Date of Issue: 27th September, 2008

OBVERSE DESCRIPTION OF COIN

Ashoka Lion Capital, denomination below, Bharat/India on sides

REVERSE DESCRIPTION OF COIN

Portait of Bhagat singh, Date-1907-2007 Below, Legend "shaheed Bhagat singh birth Centenary"

SI No	Year	Denomina-tion	Weight of the Coin	Metal Compo-sitions	Shape & Size			Mint
					Dia	Edge	Shape	
1	2007	100 Rupees	35	S50	44	Milled /200	Circular	Kolkata
2	2007	5rupees	6	Ss	23	Security/100	Circular	Kolkata

TER-CENTENARY OF GUR-TA-GUDDI OF SHRI GURU GRANTH SAHIB (2008)

Date of Issue: 30th October, 2008

OBVERSE DESCRIPTION OF COIN

Ashoka Lion Capital, denomination below, Bharat/India on sides

REVERSE DESCRIPTION OF COIN

Golden Temple date 2008 below, Legend "Ter Centenary of Gur-Ta-Gadi"

Sl No	Year	Denomina-tion	Weight of the Coin	Metal Com-positions	Shape & Size			Mint
					Dia	Edge	Shape	
1	2008	10 Rupees	7.71	Ccupro Nickel Bi-Metalic	27	Plain	Circular	Kolkata Hydrabad
2	2008	100 Rupees	35	S50	44	Milled /200	Circular	Kolkata

150 YEARS BIRTH CENTENARY ST. ALPHONSA

Date of Issue:23rd AUGUST 2009

OBVERSE DESCRIPTION OF COIN

Ashoka Lion Capital, denomination below, Bharat/India on sides

REVERSE DESCRIPTION OF COIN

Portait of Saint Alphonsa, date-1910-2009, legend "Saint Alphonsa Birth Centenary"

SI No	Year	Denomina-tion	Weight of the Coin	Metal Com-positions	Shape & Size			Mint
					Dia	Edge	Shape	
1	2009	100 Rupees	35 Gms	Quaternary Allloy	44 Mm	Milled, Serr.200	Circular	Mumbai
2	2009	5 Rupees	6 Gms	Nickel Brass	23 Mm	Milled	Circular	Mumbai

PERARIGNAR ANNA BIRTH CENTENARY (1909-1969)

Date of Issue:2009

OBVERSE DESCRIPTION OF COIN

Ashoka Lion Capital, denomination below, Bharat/India on sides

REVERSE DESCRIPTION OF COIN

Bust of Perarignar Anna,Date-1909-1969, Legend –Perarignar Anna Centenary.

Sl No	Year	Denomina-tion	Weight of the Coin	Metal Com-positions	Shape & Size			Mint
					Dia	Edge	Shape	
1	2009	100 Rupees	35 Gms	Quaternary Allloy	44 Mm	Milled, Serr.200	Circular	Mumbai
2	2009	5 Rupees	6 Gms	Nickel Brass	23 Mm	Milled	Circular	Mumbai

60th ANNIVERSARY OF COMMON WEALTH GAME

Date of Issue: 29th NOVEMBER 2009

OBVERSE DESCRIPTION OF COIN

Ashoka Lion Capital, denomination below, Bharat/India on sides

REVERSE DESCRIPTION OF COIN

Parliament Building with Flag, Date 2009 Below, Legend "60 Years of Common wealth".

Sl No	Year	Denomi- nation	Weight of the Coin	Metal Com- positions	Shape & Size			Mint
					Dia	Edge	Shape	
1	2009	100 Ru- pees	35 Gms	Quaternary Allloy	44 Mm	Milled, Serr.200	Circular	Mumbai
2	2009	5 Rupees	6 Gms	Nickel Brass	23 Mm	Milled	Circular	Mumbai

200th BIRTH ANNIVERSARY OF LOUIS BRAILLE(1809-2009)

Date of Issue:23rd AUGUST 2009

OBVERSE DESCRIPTION OF COIN

Ashoka Lion Capital, denomination below, Bharat/India on sides

REVERSE DESCRIPTION OF COIN

Bust of Luies Braille with "Louise Brallie" in Brallie chars, Date-1809-2009 Mentioned Legend 'Louise Braille"

Sl No	Year	Denomination	Weight of the Coin	Metal Compositions	Shape & Size			Mint
					Dia	Edge	Shape	
1	2009	100 Rupees	35 Gms	Quaternary Allloy	44 Mm	Milled, Serr.200	Circular	Mumbai
2	2009	2 Rupees	5.62 Gms	Ferratic Stainless Steel	27 Mm	Milled	Circular	Mumbai

DR. HOMI BHABHA BIRTH CENTENARY

Date of Issue: 29th NOVEMBER 2009

OBVERSE DESCRIPTION OF COIN

Ashoka Lion Capital, denomination below, Bharat/India on sides

REVERSE DESCRIPTION OF COIN

Bust of Homi Bhaba, Date-2008 Below, Legend "Homi Bhaba Birth Century year"

Sl No	Year	Denomina-tion	Weight of the Coin	Metal Com-positions	Shape & Size			Mint
					Dia	Edge	Shape	
1	2009	100 Rupees	35 Gms	Quaternary Allloy	44 Mm	Milled, Serr.200	Circular	Mumbai
2	2009	5 Rupees	7.71 Gms	Metalic	27 Mm	Milled	Circular	Mumbai

125ᵗʰ BIRTH ANNIVERSARY OF THE FIRST PRESIDENT OF INDIA DR. RAJENDRA PRASAD

Date of Issue: 2010

OBVERSE DESCRIPTION OF COIN

Ashoka Lion Capital, denomination below, Bharat/India on sides

REVERSE DESCRIPTION OF COIN

Bust of Homi Bhaba, Date-2008 Below, Legend "Homi Bhaba Birth Century year"

Sl No	Year	Denomina-tion	Weight of the Coin	Metal Com-positions	Shape & Size			Mint
					Dia	Edge	Shape	
1	2010	100 Rupees	35 Gms	Quaternary Alloy	44 Mm	Milled	Circular	Mumbai
2	2010	5 Rupees	6 Gms	Nickel Brass	23 Mm	Milled	Circular	Mumbai

150th BIRTH ANNIVERSARY OF RABINDRANATH TAGORE

Date of Issue: 2010

OBVERSE DESCRIPTION OF COIN

Ashoka Lion Capital, denomination below, Bharat/India on sides

REVERSE DESCRIPTION OF COIN

Bust of Rabindranath Tagore, Date 1861-2011 Below, Legend "Rabindranath Tagore 150th Birth Anniversary"

Sl No	Year	Denomination	Weight of the Coin	Metal Com-positions	Shape & Size			Mint
					Dia	Edge	Shape	
1	2010	100 Rupees	35 Gms	Quaternary Alloy	44 Mm	Milled	Circular	Mumbai
2	2010	5 Rupees	6 Gms	Nickel Brass	23 Mm	Milled	Circular	Mumbai

MOTHER TERESA BIRTH CENTENARY

Date of Issue: 2010

OBVERSE DESCRIPTION OF COIN

Ashoka Lion Capital, denomination below, Bharat/India on sides

REVERSE DESCRIPTION OF COIN

Bust of Mother Teresa, Date 1910-2010 below, Legend "Mother Teresa Birth cenetary"

Sl No	Year	Denomina-tion	Weight of the Coin	Metal Com-positions	Shape & Size			Mint
					Dia	Edge	Shape	
1	2010	100 Rupees	35 Gms	Quaternary Alloy	44 Mm	Milled	Circular	Mumbai
2	2010	5 Rupees	6 Gms	Nickel Brass	23 Mm	Milled	Circular	Mumbai

RBI PLATINUM JUBLEE CELEBRATIONS (1935-2010)

Date of Issue:28th February 2010

OBVERSE DESCRIPTION OF COIN

Ashoka Lion Capital, denomination below, Bharat/India on sides

REVERSE DESCRIPTION OF COIN

Tiger and Palm Tree, Crest of RBI, Date-1935-2010 Below, Legend Reserve Bank of India Platinum Jubilee.

Sl No	Year	Denomina-tion	Weight of the Coin	Metal Com-positions	Shape & Size			Mint
					Dia	Edge	Shape	
1	2010	75 Rupees	35 Gms	Q A	44 Mm	Milled	Circular	Mumbai
2	2010	10 Rupees	7.71 Gms	Bi-Metallic	27 Mm	Milled	Circular	Mumbai
3	2010	5 Rupees	6 Gms	Nickel Brass	23 Mm	Milled	Circular	Mumbai
4	2010	2 Rupees	5.62 Gms	Ferratic Stain-less Steel	27 Mm	Milled	Circular	Mumbai
5	2010	1 Rupees	4.82 Gms	Ferratic Stain-less Steel	25 Mm	Milled	Circular	Mumbai

C SUBHRAMANIAM BIRTH CENTENARY

Date of Issue: 2010

OBVERSE DESCRIPTION OF COIN

Ashoka Lion Capital, denomination below, Bharat/India on sides

REVERSE DESCRIPTION OF COIN

Bust of C. Subhramaniam Date-1910-2010 below, Legend" C. Subhramaniam Birth Centenary"

SI No	Year	Denomina-tion	Weight of the Coin	Metal Com-positions	Shape & Size			Mint
					Dia	Edge	Shape	
1	2010	100 rupees	35 Gms	Q A	44 Mm	Milled	Circular	Mumbai
2	2010	5 Rupees	6 Gms	Nickel-Brass	23 Mm	Milled	Circular	Mumbai

1000 YEAR OF BRIHADEESWARAR TEMPLE THANJAVUR, TAMIL NADU

Date of Issue: 26th September 2010

OBVERSE DESCRIPTION OF COIN

Ashoka Lion Capital, denomination below, Bharat/India on sides

REVERSE DESCRIPTION OF COIN

Briddheswar Temple and statue of king Raja Raja Chola in Front of Thanjavur written below date 2010 below, legend" 1000 year of Brihadeeswarar Temple"

Sl No	Year	Denomina-tion	Weight of the Coin	Metal Composi-tions	Shape & Size			Mint
					Dia	Edge	Shape	
1	2010	100 Rupees	35 Gms	Silver Copper	44 Gms	Milled	Circular	Mumbai
2	2010	5 Rupees	6 Gms	Nickel Brass	33 Gms	Milled	Circular	Mumbai

XIX COMMONWEALTH GAMES 2010, DELHI

Date of Issue: 2010

OBVERSE DESCRIPTION OF COIN

Ashoka Lion Capital, denomination below, Bharat/India on sides

REVERSE DESCRIPTION OF COIN

Logo of XIX Common Wealth Games, Date-3-14 October 2010 Below, Legend "XIX common wealth Games 2010 Delhi"

Sl No	Year	Denomina-tion	Weight of the Coin	Metal Compo-sitions	Shape & Size			Mint
					Dia	Edge	Shape	
1	2010	100 Rupees	35 Gms	Quaternary Allloy	44 Mm	Milled	Circular	Mumbai
2	2010	5 Rupees	6 Gms	Nickel Brass	23 Mm	Milled	Circular	Mumbai
3	2010	2 Coin	5.62 Gms	Ferratic Stain-less Steel	27 Mm	Milled	Circular	Mumbai

150 YEARS OF INCOME TAX

Date of Issue: 2011

OBVERSE DESCRIPTION OF COIN
Ashoka Lion Capital, denomination below, Bharat/India on sides

REVERSE DESCRIPTION OF COIN
Portrait of Chanakya and lotus with Honeybee Date-1860-2010 Below Legend" Income tax-150 of Building India "

SI No	Year	Denomina-tion	Weight of the Coin	Metal Com-positions	Shape & Size			Mint
					Dia	Edge	Shape	
1	2011	150 Rupees	35 Gms	Quaternary Allloy	44 Mm	Milled	Circular	Mumbai
2	2011	5 Rupees	6 Gms	Cupro Nickel	23 Mm	Milled	Circular	Mumbai

100 YEAR OF CIVIL AVIATION

Date of Issue: 17th October 2011

OBVERSE DESCRIPTION OF COIN

Ashoka Lion Capital, denomination below, Bharat/India on sides

REVERSE DESCRIPTION OF COIN

Aircraft and figure "100". Year with years over laping date-1911 2011 Legent" Civil Avition India"

SI No	Year	Denomina-tion	Weight of the Coin	Metal Com-positions	Shape & Size			Mint
					Dia	Edge	Shape	
1	2010	100 Rupees	35 Gms	Quaternary Allloy	44 Mm	Milled	Circular	Mumbai
2	2010	5 Rupees	6 Gms	Cupro Nickel	23 Mm	Milled	Circular	Mumbai

100 YEARS OF INDIAN COUNCIL OF MEDICAL RESEARCH (ICMR)

Date of Issue:15th November 2011

Ashoka Lion Capital, denomination below, Bharat/India on sides

REVERSE DESCRIPTION OF COIN

Emblem of ICMR flanked by "Centenary year" Date-1911-2011 Below, Legend Indian Civil for Medical Research.

Sl No	Year	Denomina-tion	Weight of the Coin	Metal Com-positions	Shape & Size			Mint
					Dia	Edge	Shape	
1	2011	100 Rupees	35 Gms	Quaternary Allloy	44 Mm	Milled	Circular	Mumbai
2	2011	5 Rupees	6 Gms	Nb	23 Mm	Milled	Circular	Mumbai

150 YEAR CAG

Date of Issue:2011

OBVERSE DESCRIPTION OF COIN

Ashoka Lion Capital, denomination below, Bharat/India on sides

REVERSE DESCRIPTION OF COIN

Logo of CAG, Date-1860-2010 Below, Legend-Comptroller and Auditor General of India [CAG]

Sl No	Year	Denomina-tion	Weight of the Coin	Metal Composi-tions	Shape & Size			Mint
					Dia	Edge	Shape	
1	2011	150 Rupees	35 Gms	Quaternary Allloy	44 Gms	Milled	Circular	Mumbai
2	2011	5 Rupees	6gms	Nb	23gms	Milled	Circular	Mumbai

60 YEARS OF KOLKATA MINT

Date of Issue: 20ᵗʰ June 2012

OBVERSE DESCRIPTION OF COIN
Ashoka Lion Capital, denomination below, Bharat/India on sides

REVERSE DESCRIPTION OF COIN
Mint Building, Date-1952-2012 Below. Legend" 60 years of India Govt.
Mint Kolkata"

Sl No	Year	Denomination	Weight of the Coin	Metal Compositions	Shape & Size			Mint
					Dia	Edge	Shape	
1	2012	60 Rupees	22.5 Gms	Quaternary Allloy	39 Mm	Milled	Circular	Kolkata
2	2012	5 Rupees	6 Gms	Cupro Nickel	23 Mm	Milled	Circular	Kolkata

60 YEARS OF PARLIAMENT OF INDIA 1952-2012

Date of Issue: 2012

OBVERSE DESCRIPTION OF COIN

Ashoka Lion Capital, denomination below, Bharat/India on sides

REVERSE DESCRIPTION OF COIN

Image of parliament with flag Date-1952-2012 Below. Legend "60 years of parliament"

SI No	Year	Denomination	Weight of the Coin	Metal Compositions	Shape & Size			Mint
					Dia	Edge	Shape	
1	2012	10 Rupees	7.71 Gms	Bi-Mettalic	27 Mm	Reeded	Circular	Mumbai
2	2012	5 Rupees	6 Gms	Nb	23 Mm	Reeded	Circular	Mumbai

150th YEAR OF KUKA MOVEMENT

Date of Issue:01st October 2012

OBVERSE DESCRIPTION OF COIN

Ashoka Lion Capital, denomination below, Bharat/India on sides

REVERSE DESCRIPTION OF COIN

Potrait of satguru ram singh ji at center his followers hanged on left standing ion front of cannon on right date-1857-2007 Below legend "150 years of Kuka Movement"

Sl No	Year	Denomination	Weight of the Coin	Metal Compositions	Shape & Size			Mint
					Dia	Edge	Shape	
1	2012	100 Rupees	35 Gms	Quaternary Allloy	44 Mm	Milled	Circular	Mumbai
2	2012	5 Rupees	6 Gms	Cupro Nickel	23 Mm	Milled	Circular	Mumbai

150th BIRTH ANNIVERSARY MOTILAL NEHRU

Date of Issue: 2012

OBVERSE DESCRIPTION OF COIN

Ashoka Lion Capital, denomination below, Bharat/India on sides

REVERSE DESCRIPTION OF COIN

Bust of Motilal Nehru Date 2012 Below, Legend "150th Birth Anniversary Motilal Nehru"

Sl No	Year	Denomination	Weight of the Coin	Metal Compositions	Shape & Size			Mint
					Dia	Edge	Shape	
1	2012	150 Rupees	35 Gms	Quaternary Allloy	44 Mm	Milled	Circular	Mumbai
2	2012	5 Rupees	6 Gms	Nb	23 Mm	Milled	Circular	Mumbai

150th BIRTH ANNIVERSARY OF MADAN MOHAN MALAVIYA (2012)

Date of Issue: 2012

OBVERSE DESCRIPTION OF COIN

Ashoka Lion Capital, denomination below, Bharat/India on sides

REVERSE DESCRIPTION OF COIN

Bust of Madan Mohan Malaviya Date-1861-2011 Below, Legend "150th Birth Anniversary Madan Mohan Malaviya"

Sl No	Year	Denomination	Weight of the Coin	Metal Compositions	Shape & Size			Mint
					Dia	Edge	Shape	
1	2012	150 Rupees	35 Gms	Quaternary Allloy	44 Gms	Milled	Circular	Mumbai
2	2012	5 Rupees	6 Gms	Nb	23 Gms	Milled	Circular	Mumbai

SILVER JUBLIEE OF SHRI MATA VAISHNOV DEVI SHRINE BOARD

Date of Issue:31st January 2013

OBVERSE DESCRIPTION OF COIN

Ashoka Lion Capital, denomination below, Bharat/India on sides

REVERSE DESCRIPTION OF COIN

Picture of Shri mata Vaishnodevi Date 2012 Below, Legend "Shri Mata Vaishno Devi Shrine Board"

SI No	Year	Denomina-tion	Weight of the Coin	Metal Com-positions	Shape & Size			Mint
					Dia	Edge	Shape	
1	2013	25 Rupees	35 Gms	Quaternary Allloy	44 Gms	Reeded	Circular	Mumbai
2	2013	10 Rupees	7.71 Gms	Nb	27 Gms	Smooth	Circular	Mumbai
3	2013	5 Rupees	6 Gms	Cupro Nickel	23 Gms	Smooth	Circular	Mumbai

150 BIRTH ANNIVERSARY OF SWAMI VIVEKANANDA (1863-1902)

Date of Issue:31ˢᵗ January 2013

OBVERSE DESCRIPTION OF COIN

Ashoka Lion Capital, denomination below, Bharat/India on sides

REVERSE DESCRIPTION OF COIN

Bust of Swami Vivekananda Date-1863 on left and 1902 on right Legend "150th Birth Anniversary Swami Vivekananda"

Sl No	Year	Denomina-tion	Weight of the Coin	Metal Com-positions	Shape & Size			Mint
					Dia	Edge	Shape	
1	2013	150 Rupees	35 Gms	Quaternary Allloy	44 Mm	Milled	Circular	Kolkata
2	2013	5 Rupees	6 Gms	Nb	23 Mm	Milled	Circular	Kolkata

MOULANA ABUL KALAM AZAD

Date of Issue:2013

OBVERSE DESCRIPTION OF COIN

Ashoka Lion Capital, denomination below, Bharat/India on sides

REVERSE DESCRIPTION OF COIN

Bust of Maulana Abul kalam Azad Date-1888-1958, Legend "125th Anniversary Maulana Abul Kalam Azad"

Sl No	Year	Denomina-tion	Weight of the Coin	Metal Com-positions	Shape & Size			Mint
					Dia	Edge	Shape	
1	2013	20 Rupees	30 Gms	Quaternary Allloy	39 Mm	Milled	Circular	Kolkata
2	2013	5 Rupees	6 Gms	Nb	23 Mm	Milled	Circular	Kolkata

ACHARYA TULSI BIRTH CENTENARY

Date of Issue:2014

OBVERSE DESCRIPTION OF COIN

Ashoka Lion Capital, denomination below, Bharat/India on sides

REVERSE DESCRIPTION OF COIN

Bust of Acharya Tulasi Date-1914-2013 Below, Legend "Achary Tulai Birth Centenary"

Sl No	Year	Denomi-nation	Weight of the Coin	Metal Com-positions	Shape & Size			Mint
					Dia	Edge	Shape	
1	2013	20 Rupees	30 Gms	Quaternary Allloy	39 Mm	Milled	Circular	Kolkata
2	2013	5 Rupees	6 Gms	Nb	23 Mm	Milled	Circular	Kolkata

60 YEARS OF COIR BOARD

OBVERSE DESCRIPTION OF COIN

Ashoka Lion Capital, denomination below, Bharat/India on sides

REVERSE DESCRIPTION OF COIN

Logo of Coir Board Date-1953-2013 Legend "60 years of Coir Board"

Sl No	Year	Denomination	Weight of the Coin	Metal Compositions	Shape & Size			Mint
					Dia	Edge	Shape	
1	2014	60 Rupees	35 Gms	Quaternary Allloy	44 Mm	Milled	Circular	Mumbai
2	2014	10 Rupees	7.71 Gms	Bi-Mettalic	27 Mm	Milled	Circular	Mumbai

CENTURY OF KOMAGATA MARU INCIDENT

Date of Issue: 2014

OBVERSE DESCRIPTION OF COIN

Ashoka Lion Capital, denomination below, Bharat/India on sides

REVERSE DESCRIPTION OF COIN

Komagata Maru Ship Date 1914-2014 Below, Legend" Cenetary Celebration Komagatamaru Incident"

Sl No	Year	Denomina-tion	Weight of the Coin	Metal Composi-tions	Shape & Size			Mint
					Dia	Edge	Shape	
1	2015	100 Rupees	35 Gms	Quaternary Allloy	44 Mm	Milled	Circular	Mumbai
2	2015	5 Rupees	6 Gms	Nb	23 Smm	Milled	Circular	Mumbai

BEGUM AKHTAR OF BIRTH CEMTENARY

Date of Issue: 2014

OBVERSE DESCRIPTION OF COIN

Ashoka Lion Capital, denomination below, Bharat/India on sides

REVERSE DESCRIPTION OF COIN

Bust of Begum Akhtar Date-1914 2014 below, Legend Birth Century of Begum Akhtar"

Sl No	Year	Denomina-tion	Weight of the Coin	Metal Com-positions	Shape & Size			Mint
					Dia	Edge	Shape	
1	2014	100 Rupees	35 Gms	Quaternary Allloy	44 Mm	Milled	Circular	Mumbai
2	2014	5 Rupees	6 Gms	Nb	23 Smm	Milled	Circular	Mumbai

125th BIRTH ANNIVERSARY OF JAWHARLAL NEHRU

Date of Issue: 2014

OBVERSE DESCRIPTION OF COIN

Ashoka Lion Capital, denomination below, Bharat/India on sides

REVERSE DESCRIPTION OF COIN

Bust of Jawaharlal Nehru, Date 1889-2014 below, Legend "125th Birth Anniversary of Jawaharlal Nehru"

Sl No	Year	Denomination	Weight of the Coin	Metal Compositions	Shape & Size			Mint
					Dia	Edge	Shape	
1	2014	125 Rupees	35 Gms	Quaternary Allloy	44 Mm	Milled	Circular	Mumbai
2	2014	5 Rupees	6 Gms	Nb	23 Smm	Milled	Circular	Mumbai

JAMSETJI NUSSERWANJI TATA

Date of Issue: 2015

OBVERSE DESCRIPTION OF COIN

Ashoka Lion Capital, denomination with Rupee Symbol Bharat/India on sides

REVERSE DESCRIPTION OF COIN

Bust of Jamsetji Tata, Date 1839-2014 below, Legend "175th Birth Anniversary jamsetji Nusserwanji-Tata"

SI No	Year	Denomi-nation	Weight of the Coin	Metal Com-positions	Shape & Size			Mint
					Dia	Edge	Shape	
1	2014	100 Rupees	35 Gms	Silver (500)	44 Mm	Milled	Circular	Kolkata
2	2014	5 Rupees	6 Grams	Nickel-Brass	23 Mm	100 Setations	Circular	Kolkata

50 YEARS OF BHEL

Date of Issue: 2015

OBVERSE DESCRIPTION OF COIN

Ashoka Lion Capital, denomination with Rupee Symbol Bharat/India on sides

REVERSE DESCRIPTION OF COIN

Logo of Golden Jubliee of BHEL at Centre, Date-1964-2014, Below, Legend "50 Years of Engineering Excellence"

SI No	Year	Denomina-tion	Weight of the Coin	Metal Com-positions	Shape & Size			Mint
					Dia	Edge	Shape	
1	2014	50 Rupees	35 Gms	Quaternary Allloy	44 Mm	Milled	Circular	Kolkata
2	2014	5 Rupees	6 Gms	Nickel-Brass	23 Mm	100 Se-tations	Circular	Kolkata

CENTENARY OF MAHATMA GANDHI'S RETURN FROM SOUTH AFRICA

Date of Issue:08th January 2015

OBVERSE DESCRIPTION OF COIN

Ashoka Lion Capital, denomination with Rupee Symbol Bharat/India on sides

REVERSE DESCRIPTION OF COIN

Dual Portait of Mahatma Gandhi, Date-1915-2015 below, Legend "Mahatma Gandhi Return from South africa Centenary Commemoration"

SI No	Year	Denomina-tion	Weight of the Coin	Metal Com-positions	Shape & Size			Mint
					Dia	Edge	Shape	
1	2015	100 Rupees	35 Gms	Q A	44 Mm	Milled	Circular	Mumbai
2	2015	10 Rupees	7.71 Gms	Bi-Mettalic	27 Mm	Milled	Circular	Mumbai

SWAMI CHINMAYANANDA

Date of Issue: 2015

OBVERSE DESCRIPTION OF COIN
Ashoka Lion Capital, denomination with Rupee Symbol Bharat/India on sides

REVERSE DESCRIPTION OF COIN
Bust of swami Chinmayananda Date 2015 Below, Legend "Birth Centenary of Swami Chinmayananda"

SI No	Year	Denomination	Weight of the Coin	Metal Compositions	Shape & Size			Mint
					Dia	Edge	Shape	
1	2015	100 Rupees	35 Gms	Quaternary Allloy	44 Mm	Reeded	Circular	Kolkata
2	2015	10 Rupees	7.71 Gms	Bi-Metallic	27 Mm	Bi-Mettalic	Circular	Kolkata

INTERNATIONAL YOGA DAY

Date of Issue: 2015

OBVERSE DESCRIPTION OF COIN

Ashoka Lion Capital, denomination with Rupee Symbol Bharat/India on sides

REVERSE DESCRIPTION OF COIN

Logo with Yoga posture, Date-21th June, year 2015 Below, Legend "International Day of Yoga, yoga for Harmony & Peace"

SI No	Year	Denomina-tion	Weight of the Coin	Metal Composi-tions	Shape & Size			Mint
					Dia	Edge	Shape	
1	2015	100 Rupees	35 Gms	Quaternary Allloy	44 Mm	Milled	Circular	Mumbai
2	2015	10 Rupees	7.71 Gms	Bi-Mettalic	27 Mm	Milled	Circular	Mumbai

RANI GAIDINLIU BIRTH CENTENARY

Date of Issue:06th December 2015

OBVERSE DESCRIPTION OF COIN

Ashoka Lion Capital, denomination with Rupee Symbol Bharat/India on sides

REVERSE DESCRIPTION OF COIN

Bust of Rani Gaidinilu Date-1915-2015 below Legend "Birth Cenetaray of Gaidinliu"

SI No	Year	Denomina-tion	Weight of the Coin	Metal Com-positions	Shape & Size			Mint
					Dia	Edge	Shape	
1	2015	100 Rupees	35 Gms	Quaternary Allloy	44 Mm	Plain	Circular	Mumbai
2	2015	10 Rupees	7.71 Gms	Bi-Mettalic	27 Mm	Plain	Circular	Mumbai

125th BIRTH ANNIVERSARY OF DR. S RADHAKRISHNAN

Date of Issue: 2015

OBVERSE DESCRIPTION OF COIN

Ashoka Lion Capital, denomination with Rupee Symbol Bharat/India on sides

REVERSE DESCRIPTION OF COIN

Bust of Dr. Sarvepalli Radhakrishnan Date-2015 below Legend "125th Birth Anniversary of Dr. S Radha Krishnan"

Sl No	Year	Denomina-tion	Weight of the Coin	Metal Composi-tions	Shape & Size			Mint
					Dia	Edge	Shape	
1	2015	125 Rupees	35 Gms	Quaternary Allloy	44 Mm	Plain	Circular	Mumbai
2	2015	10 Rupees	7.71 Gms	Bi-Mettalic	27 Mm	Plain	Circular	Mumbai

GOLDEN JUBILEE OF 1965 OPERATION

Date of Issue: 2015

OBVERSE DESCRIPTION OF COIN

Ashoka Lion Capital, denomination with Rupee Symbol Bharat/India on sides

REVERSE DESCRIPTION OF COIN

Amar Jawan Monument along Olive leaves, Date-2015 below, Legend "Golden Jubliee 1965 Operation"

Sl No	Year	Denomina-tion	Weight of the Coin	Metal Composi-tions	Shape & Size			Mint
					Dia	Edge	Shape	
1	2015	50 Rupees	35 Gms	Quaternary Allloy	44 Mm	Plain	Circular	Mumbai
2	2015	5 Rupees	6 Gms	Nb	23 Mm	Plain	Circular	Mumbai

3rd INDIA AFRICA SUMMIT

Date of Issue: 2015

OBVERSE DESCRIPTION OF COIN
Ashoka Lion Capital, denomination with Rupee Symbol Bharat/India on sides

REVERSE DESCRIPTION OF COIN
Logo of India Africa Summit: Face of lion with overlapping maps of india and Africa, Date-2015 Below, Legend "3rd India-Africa Forum Summit"

Sl No	Year	Denomination	Weight of the Coin	Metal Compositions	Shape & Size			Mint
					Dia	Edge	Shape	
1	2015	500 Rupees	35 Gms	Simer (500)	44	200 Serrations	Circular	Kolkata
2	2015	10 Rupees	7.71 Gms	Nickel Brass	23	100 Serrations	Circular	Kolkata

DR. BR AMBEDKAR – 125th BIRTH ANNIVERSARY

Date of Issue: 2015

OBVERSE DESCRIPTION OF COIN

Ashoka Lion Capital, denomination with Rupee Symbol Bharat/India on sides

REVERSE DESCRIPTION OF COIN

Bust of Dr. B.R. Ambedkar, Date-2015 Below, Legend "125th Birth Anniversary of Dr. B R. Ambedkar

SI No	Year	Denomination	Weight of the Coin	Metal Compositions	Shape & Size			Mint
					Dia	Edge	Shape	
1	2015	125 Rupees	35 Gms	Quaternary Allloy	44 Mm	Milled	Circular	Mumbai
2	2015	10 Rupees	7.71 Gms	Bi-Mettalic	27 Mm	Milled	Circular	Mumbai

150th BIRTH ANNIVERSARY OF LALA LAJPAT RAI

Date of Issue: 2016

OBVERSE DESCRIPTION OF COIN

Ashoka Lion Capital, denomination with Rupee Symbol Bharat/India on sides

REVERSE DESCRIPTION OF COIN

Bust of Lala Lajpat Rai, Date-1865-2015 Below, Legend "150th Birth Anniversary of Lala Lajpath Rai"

Sl No	Year	Denomina-tion	Weight of the Coin	Metal Composi-tions	Shape & Size			Mint
					Dia	Edge	Shape	
1	2016	150 Rupees	35	Q A	44	200 Settations	Circular	Kolkata
2	2016	10 Rupees	7.71	Bi-Mettalic	27	Plain	Circular	Kolkata

BIJU PATNIAK BIRTH CENTENARY

Date of Issue: 2016

OBVERSE DESCRIPTION OF COIN

Ashoka Lion Capital, denomination with Rupee Symbol Bharat/India on sides

REVERSE DESCRIPTION OF COIN

Bust of Biju Patnaik Date-1916-2016 Below, Legend "Biju Patnaik Birth Century"

| SI No | Year | Denomina-tion | Weight of the Coin | Metal Com-positions | Shape & Size | | | Mint |
					Dia	Edge	Shape	
1	2016	100 Rupees	35	Quaternary Allloy	44	200 Setta-tions	Circular	Kolkata
2	2016	5 Rupees	6	Nb	23	Plain	Circular	Kolkata

NATIONAL ARCHIVES OF INDIA

Date of Issue: 2016

OBVERSE DESCRIPTION OF COIN

Ashoka Lion Capital, denomination with Rupee Symbol Bharat/India on sides

REVERSE DESCRIPTION OF COIN

Image of National Archives Building with 125 years and logo of 125 years celebrations, date 1891-2016 Mentioned, Legend "National Archives of India"

SI No	Year	Denomina-tion	Weight of the Coin	Metal Com-positions	Shape & Size			Mint
					Dia	Edge	Shape	
1	2016	125 Rupees	37	Quaternary Allloy	44	200 Serrations	Circular	Mumbai
2	2016	10 Rupees	7.71	B M	27	Plain	Circular	Mumbai

ALLAHABAD HIGH COURT

Date of Issue: 2016

OBVERSE DESCRIPTION OF COIN

Ashoka Lion Capital, denomination with Rupee Symbol Bharat/India on sides

REVERSE DESCRIPTION OF COIN

Center Façade of Allahabad High Court emerging from the book, Date-1866-2016 Below. Legend "150th Anniversary of Allahabad High Court"

Sl No	Year	Denomination	Weight of the Coin	Metal Compositions	Shape & Size			Mint
					Dia	Edge	Shape	
1	2016	150 Rupees	35	Quaternary Allloy	44	Reeded	Circular	Mumbai
2	2016	5 Rupees	6	Nichel Brass	23	Reeded	Circular	Mumbai

TATYA TOPE – 200ᵗʰ BIRTH ANNIVERASRY

Date of Issue: 2016

OBVERSE DESCRIPTION OF COIN
Ashoka Lion Capital, denomination with Rupee Symbol Bharat/India on sides

REVERSE DESCRIPTION OF COIN
Portait of Tatya Tope Date 2015 Below "2000 Birth Centenary Of Tatya Tope"

SI No	Year	Denomi-nation	Weight of the Coin	Metal Com-positions	Shape & Size			Mint
					Dia	Edge	Shape	
1	2016	200 Rupees	35	Quaternary Allloy	44	Reeded With 200 Serrations	Circular	Kolkata
2	2016	10 Rupees	7.71	Bi-Mettalic	27	Milled	Circular	Kolkata

MAHARANA PRATAP 475th BIRTH ANNIVERSARY

Date of Issue:2016

OBVERSE DESCRIPTION OF COIN

Ashoka Lion Capital, denomination with Rupee Symbol Bharat/India on sides

REVERSE DESCRIPTION OF COIN

Portrait of Moharana Pratap date 2015 Below, Legend "475th Birth Anniversary of Moharana Pratap"

Sl No	Year	Denomination	Weight of the Coin	Metal Compositions	Shape & Size			Mint
					Dia	Edge	Shape	
1	2016	100 Rupees	35	Quaternary Allloy	44	Reeded With 200 Serrations	Circular	Mumbai
2	2016	10 Ruees	7.71	Bm	27	Reeded With 200 Serrations	Circular	Mumbai

BANARAS HINDU UNIVERSITY

Date of Issue:2016

OBVERSE DESCRIPTION OF COIN

Ashoka Lion Capital, denomination with Rupee Symbol Bharat/India on sides

REVERSE DESCRIPTION OF COIN

Logo of Banaras University Date 1916-2016 Mentioned, Legend "Centenary Year. Banaras Hindu University"

SI No	Year	Denomination	Weight of the Coin	Metal Compositions	Shape & Size			Mint
					Dia	Edge	Shape	
1	2016	100 Rupees	35	Quaternary Allloy	44	Reeded With 200 Serrations	Circular	Mumbai
2	2016	10 Rupees	7.71	Bm	27	Reeded With 200 Serrations	Circular	Mumbai

SHRI KRISHNA CHAITANYA MAHAPRABHU

Date of Issue: 2016

OBVERSE DESCRIPTION OF COIN

Ashoka Lion Capital, denomination with Rupee Symbol Bharat/India on sides

REVERSE DESCRIPTION OF COIN

Image of Shri Krishna Chaitanya Mahaprabhu date 2015 Below, Legend "500th Aniversary of Shri Krishna Chaitanya Mahaprabhu's coming to VRindaban"

SI No	Year	Denomination	Weight of the Coin	Metal Compositions	Shape & Size			Mint
					Dia	Edge	Shape	
1	2017	500 Rupees	35	Q A	44 Mm	Milled	Circular	Kolkata
2	2017	10 Rupees	7.71	B M	27 Mm	Milled	Circular	Kolkata

UNIVERSITY OF MYSORE CENTENARY CELEBRATION

Date of Issue: 2016

OBVERSE DESCRIPTION OF COIN

Ashoka Lion Capital, denomination with Rupee Symbol Bharat/India on sides

REVERSE DESCRIPTION OF COIN

Image of Crow Frod Hall along with Bust of Shri Sri Krishna Raja Wadeyar IV, Date-1916-2016 mentioned. Legend" University of Mysore Centenary Celebration"

Sl No	Year	Denomina-tion	Weight of the Coin	Metal Com-positions	Shape & Size			Mint
					Dia	Edge	Shape	
1	2016	100 Rupees	35	Quaternary Allloy	44	Reeded With 200 Serrations	Circular	Mumbai
2	2016	5 Rupees	6	Nb	23	Reeded With 200 Serrations	Circular	Mumbai

SHRIMAD RAJCHANDRA

Date of Issue: 2017

OBVERSE DESCRIPTION OF COIN

Ashoka Lion Capital, denomination with Rupee Symbol Bharat/India on sides

REVERSE DESCRIPTION OF COIN

Bust of Shrimad Rajachandra, Date-1867-1901 mentioned, Legend" Shrimad Rajchandra: Birth Anniversary"

SI No	Year	Denomina-tion	Weight of the Coin	Metal Com-positions	Shape & Size			Mint
					Dia	Edge	Shape	
1	2017	150 Rupees	35	Quaternary Allloy	44	Milled	Non Circular	Kolkata
2	2017	10 Rupees	7.71	Bi-Mettalic	27	Milled	Circular	Kolkata

DR. M.S SUBBULAKSHMI

Date of Issue: 2017

OBVERSE DESCRIPTION OF COIN

Ashoka Lion Capital, denomination with Rupee Symbol Bharat/India on sides

REVERSE DESCRIPTION OF COIN

Bust of Dr. M.S Subhulakshmi, Date-1916-2016 mentioned, Legend of "Birth Centeneray of Dr. Ms Subhalakshmi"

SI No	Year	Denomination	Weight of the Coin	Metal Compositions	Shape & Size			Mint
					Dia	Edge	Shape	
1	2017	100 Rupees	35	Quaternary Allloy	44	Milled	Circular	Mumbai
2	2017	10 Rupees	7.71	Bi-Mettalic	27	Milled	Circular	Mumbai

PANDIT DEENDAYAL UPADHYAYA

Date of Issue: 2017

OBVERSE DESCRIPTION OF COIN

Ashoka Lion Capital, denomination with Rupee Symbol Bharat/India on sides

REVERSE DESCRIPTION OF COIN

Bust of Pandit Deendayal Upadhaya Date-1916-2016 mentioned, Legend of "Birth Centeneray of Dr. Ms Subhalakshmi"

Sl No	Year	Denomi- nation	Weight of the Coin	Metal Com- positions	Shape & Size			Mint
					Dia	Edge	Shape	
1	2017	100 Rupees	35	Quaternary Allloy	44	Milled	Circular	Mumbai
2	2017	5 Rupees	6	Nb	23	Milled	Circular	Mumbai

SHRI JAGANNATH NABAKALEBARA

Date of Issue: 2018

OBVERSE DESCRIPTION OF COIN

Ashoka Lion Capital, denomination with Rupee Symbol Bharat/India on sides

REVERSE DESCRIPTION OF COIN

Image of Shree Jagannath at center with neelachakra Symbal Date 2015mentioned' Legend "Shree Jagannath Nabekalebara"

SI No	Year	Denomina-tion	Weight of the Coin	Metal Com-positions	Shape & Size			Mint
					Dia	Edge	Shape	
1	2018	1000 Rupees	35	Silver 80% Copper 20%	44	Milled	Circular	Mumbai
2	2018	10 Rupees	7.71	Bm	27	Milled	Circular	Mumbai

PRASANTA CHANDRA MAHALONOBIS

Date of Issue: 2018

OBVERSE DESCRIPTION OF COIN

Ashoka Lion Capital, denomination with Rupee Symbol Bharat/India on sides

REVERSE DESCRIPTION OF COIN

Bust of P.C. Mahalanobis with indian statics Symbol, Date 1893-1972 Below, Legend "125th Birth Anniversary of Prasanta Chandra Mahalonobis"

Sl No	Year	Denomina-tion	Weight of the Coin	Metal Com-positions	Shape & Size			Mint
					Dia	Edge	Shape	
1	2018	125 Rupees	35	Quaternary Allloy	44	Milled	Circular	Kolkata
2	2018	05 Rupees	6	Nickel Brass	23	Milled	Circular	Kolkata

ATAL BIHARI VAJPAYEE

Date of Issue: 2018

OBVERSE DESCRIPTION OF COIN
Ashoka Lion Capital, denomination with Rupee Symbol Bharat/India on sides

REVERSE DESCRIPTION OF COIN
Potrait of Atal Bihari Vajpayee Date-1924-2018 below, Legend "Atal Bihari Vajpayee"

SI No	Year	Denomina-tion	Weight of the Coin	Metal Com-positions	Shape & Size			Mint
					Dia	Edge	Shape	
1	2018	100 Rupees	35	Quaternary Allloy	44	Milled	Circular	Kolkata

BI – CENTENARY OF PAIKA BIDROHA

Date of Issue: 2018

OBVERSE DESCRIPTION OF COIN

Ashoka Lion Capital, denomination with Rupee Symbol Bharat/India on sides

REVERSE DESCRIPTION OF COIN

Image of "Bakshi Jagabandhu" riding the horse, Date 1817-2017 mentioned Legend "Bicenetary of Paika Bidroh"

SI No	Year	Denomination	Weight of the Coin	Metal Compositions	Shape & Size			Mint
					Dia	Edge	Shape	
1	2018	200 Rupees	35	Quaternary Allloy	44	Milled	Circular	Mumbai

75 YEARS OF TRICOLOUR

Date of Issue: 2018

OBVERSE DESCRIPTION OF COIN

Ashoka Lion Capital, denomination with Rupee Symbol Bharat/India on sides

REVERSE DESCRIPTION OF COIN

Portarait of "Netaji Subash Chandra Bose "Saluting the flag on the background of cellular Jail, Date – 30-12-1943 to 30-12-2018 below legend "First Flag Hoisting Day"

Sl No	Year	Denomina-tion	Weight of the Coin	Metal Com-positions	Shape & Size			Mint
					Dia	Edge	Shape	
1	2018	125 Rupees	35	Quaternary Allloy	44	Milled	Circular	Kolkata
2	2018	5 Rupees	6	Nickel Brass	23	Milled	Circular	Kolkata

SHRI GURU GOBIND SINGH

Date of Issue: 2019

OBVERSE DESCRIPTION OF COIN
Ashoka Lion Capital, denomination with Rupee Symbol Bharat/India on sides

REVERSE DESCRIPTION OF COIN
Takht Shri Harimandir Ji Patna Sahib in Centre Date-1666-2016 on left and right side legend "350th Prakash Utsav of Shri Guru Gobinda Singh Ji"

Sl No	Year	Denomination	Weight of the Coin	Metal Compositions	Shape & Size			Mint
					Dia	Edge	Shape	
1	2019	350 Rupees	35	Quaternary Allloy	44	Milled	Circular	Mumbai

DR. M.G. RAMACHANDRAN BIRTH CENTENARY

Date of Issue: 2019

OBVERSE DESCRIPTION OF COIN

Ashoka Lion Capital, denomination with Rupee Symbol Bharat/India on sides

REVERSE DESCRIPTION OF COIN

Bust of Dr. Ramchandran Date 1917-2017 Below, legend Dr. M.G Ramchandran Birth Century"

Sl No	Year	Denomination	Weight of the Coin	Metal Compositions	Shape & Size			Mint
					Dia	Edge	Shape	
1	2019	100 Rupees	35	Quaternary Allloy	44	Milled	Circular	Mumbai
2	2019	05 Rupees	6	N.b	23	Milled	Circular	Mumbai

JALLIANWALA BAGH MASSACRE

Date of Issue: 2019

OBVERSE DESCRIPTION OF COIN

Ashoka Lion Capital, denomination with Rupee Symbol Bharat/India on sides

REVERSE DESCRIPTION OF COIN

Jallianwala bagh Moument Date 2019 Below, Legend "Cenetary of Jallinwal bagh Massacre"

Sl No	Year	Denomina-tion	Weight of the Coin	Metal Com-positions	Shape & Size			Mint
					Dia	Edge	Shape	
1	2019	100 Rupees	35	Quaternary Allloy	44	Milled	Circular	Mumbai

VIKRAM SARABHAI BIRTH CENTENARY

Date of Issue: 2019

OBVERSE DESCRIPTION OF COIN

Ashoka Lion Capital, denomination with Rupee Symbol Bharat/India on sides

REVERSE DESCRIPTION OF COIN

Bust of Vikram Sarabhai Date-1919-2019 Legend "Vikram Sarabhai Birth Cenetenary Year"

SI No	Year	Denomina-tion	Weight of the Coin	Metal Com-positions	Shape & Size			Mint
					Dia	Edge	Shape	
1	2019	100 Rupees	35	Quaternary Allloy	44	Milled	Circular	Mumbai

150 YEARS OF MAHATMA GANDHI

Date of Issue: 2019

OBVERSE DESCRIPTION OF COIN

Ashoka Lion Capital, denomination with Rupee Symbol Bharat/India on sides

REVERSE DESCRIPTION OF COIN

Logo of 150 Years of Celebrating the mahatma date-1869-2019 Mentioned, Legend "150th Birth Anniversary of Mahatma Gandhi"

Sl No	Year	Denomination	Weight of the Coin	Metal Compo-sitions	Shape & Size			Mint
					Dia	Edge	Shape	
1	2019	150 Rupees	40	Silver	44	Milled	Circular	Mumbai

PARAMAHANSA YOGANANDA

Date of Issue:2019

OBVERSE DESCRIPTION OF COIN
Ashoka Lion Capital, denomination with Rupee Symbol Bharat/India on sides

REVERSE DESCRIPTION OF COIN
Portrait of Paramahansa Yogananda, Date-1893-2018 Below, Legend "125th Birth Anniversary of Paramhansa Yogananda"

SI No	Year	Denomination	Weight of the Coin	Metal Compositions	Shape & Size			Mint
					Dia	Edge	Shape	
1	2019	125 Rupees	35	Quaternary Allloy	44	Milled	Circular	Mumbai

GURU NANAK DEV JI 550th PRAKASH PURAB

Date of Issue: 2019

OBVERSE DESCRIPTION OF COIN

Ashoka Lion Capital, denomination with Rupee Symbol Bharat/India on sides

REVERSE DESCRIPTION OF COIN

Picture of Gurudwara Sri Ber Sahib, Sultanpur Lodhi, Punjab Date Mentioned 1469-2019, Legend "550th Prakash Purab of Shri Guru nanak Dev Ji"

Sl No	Year	Denomina-tion	Weight of the Coin	Metal Com-positions	Shape & Size			Mint
					Dia	Edge	Shape	
1	2019	550 Rupees	44	Quaternary Allloy	35	Milled	Circular	Mumbai

250th SESSION OF RAJYA SABHA

Date of Issue: 2020

OBVERSE DESCRIPTION OF COIN
Ashoka Lion Capital, denomination with Rupee Symbol Bharat/India on sides

REVERSE DESCRIPTION OF COIN
Picture of parliament house with national flag on top and seating arrangement of Rajya Sabha Chamber along with the Portait of Mahtma Gandhi" Date Mentioned 2019, Legend "250th Session of Rajya Sabha"

SI No	Year	Denomina-tion	Weight of the Coin	Metal Com-positions	Shape & Size			Mint
					Dia	Edge	Shape	
1	2020	250 Rupees	40	Quaternary Allloy	44	Milled	Circular	Mumbai

₹

SMT. VIJAYA RAJE SCINDIA

Date of Issue: 2020

OBVERSE DESCRIPTION OF COIN

Ashoka Lion Capital, denomination with Rupee Symbol Bharat/India on sides

REVERSE DESCRIPTION OF COIN

Bust of Smt. Vijay Raje Scindia, Date 1919-2019 Below, Legend "Birth Cenetary of Smt. Vijaya Raje Sindhe"

Sl No	Year	Denomination	Weight of the Coin	Metal Compositions	Shape & Size			Mint
					Dia	Edge	Shape	
1	2020	100 Rupees	35	Quaternary Allloy	44	Milled	Circular	Mumbai

75 YEARS OF FOOD & ORGANISATION

Date of Issue: 2020

OBVERSE DESCRIPTION OF COIN
Ashoka Lion Capital, denomination with Rupee Symbol Bharat/India on sides

REVERSE DESCRIPTION OF COIN
Sun Above, Lotus Flower Below, Wheat ears on either sides with Year 2020 Below Legend "sahee Poshan Desh Roshan" in Hindi.

SI No	Year	Denomina-tion	Weight of the Coin	Metal Com-positions	Shape & Size			Mint
					Dia	Edge	Shape	
1	2020	75 Rupees	35	Quaternary Allloy	44	Milled	Circular	Mumbai

125th DEPARTURE ANNIVERSARY OF SRI SHYAMACHARAN LAHIREE MAHASAYA(2020)

Date of Issue: 24th October 2020

OBVERSE DESCRIPTION OF COIN

Ashoka Lion Capital Denomination with Rupee Symbol Bharat /India on Sides

REVERSE DESCRIPTION OF COIN

Image of Sri Shyamacharan Lahiree Mahasaya, Date 1895-2020 Mentioned Legend "125th Departure Anniversary of Sri Shyamacharan Lahiree Mahasaya"

Sl No	Year	Denomi-nation	Weight of the Coin	Metal Com-positions	Shape & Size			Mint
					Dia	Edge	Shape	
1	2020	125rupees	35 Gms	Quaternary Allloy	44 Mm	Milled	Circular	Mumbai

CELEBRATION OF UNIVERSITY OF LUCKNOW (2020)

Date of Issue: 25th November 2020

OBVERSE DESCRIPTION OF COIN

Ashoka Lion Capital Denomination with Rupee Symbol Bharat /India on Sides

REVERSE DESCRIPTION OF COIN

Image of University of Lucknow building's front façade, Date 1920-2020 Mentioned, Legend "Centennial Celebration; University of Lucknow"

Sl No	Year	Denomination	Weight of the Coin	Metal Compositions	Shape & Size			Mint
					Dia	Edge	Shape	
1	2020	100 Rupees	35 Gms	Quaternary Allloy	44 Mm	Milled	Circular	Mumbai

125th BIRTH ANNIVERSARY YEAR OF NETAJI SUBHAS CHANDRA BOSE

Date of Issue: 23rd JAN 2021

OBVERSE DESCRIPTION OF COIN

Ashoka Lion Capital Denomination with Rupee Symbol Bharat /India on Sides

REVERSE DESCRIPTION OF COIN

Bust of Netaji Subhas Chandra Bose,Legend "125th Birth Anniversary Year of Netaji Subhas Chandra Bose" with year 2021 below.

SI No	Year	Denomina-tion	Weight of the Coin	Metal Com-positions	Shape & Size			Mint
					Dia	Edge	Shape	
1	2021	125 Rupees	35 Gms	Quaternary Allloy	44 Mm	Milled	Circular	Mumbai

SRILA A.C. BHAKTIVEDANTA SWAMI PRABHUPADA

Date of Issue: 01 SEPT 2021

OBVERSE DESCRIPTION OF COIN

Ashoka Lion Capital Denomination with Rupee Symbol Bharat/India on Sides

REVERSE DESCRIPTION OF COIN

Portrait of Srila Prabhupada, Legend "125th Birth Anniversary of Srila A. C. Bhaktivedanta Swami Prabhupada" with year 1896-2021.

Sl No	Year	Denomination	Weight of the Coin	Metal Compositions	Shape & Size			Mint
					Dia	Edge	Shape	
1	2021	125 Rupees	35 Gms	Quaternary Allloy	44 Mm	Milled	Circular	Kolkata

HARCOURT BUTTLER TECHNICAL UNIVERSITY

Date of Issue: 25 NOV 2021

OBVERSE DESCRIPTION OF COIN

Ashoka Lion Capital Denomination with Rupee Symbol as Bharat /India on Sides

REVERSE DESCRIPTION OF COIN

Image of Harcourt Butler Technical University, Kanpur main building, Date 1921-2021 Mentioned Legend "Harcourt Butler Technical University Kanpur Centenary Celebrations"

Sl No	Year	Denomina-tion	Weight of the Coin	Metal Composi-tions	Shape & Size			Mint
					Dia	Edge	Shape	
1	2021	100 Rupees	35 G	Quaternary Alloy	44 Mm	Milled	Circular	Kolkata

KAVI MUDDANA

Date of Issue: 2022

OBVERSE DESCRIPTION OF COIN

Ashoka Lion Capital Denomination with Rupee Symbol as Bharat/India on Sides

REVERSE DESCRIPTION OF COIN

Portait of Kavi Mundana Legend "150th Birth Anniversary of Kavi Muddana with year 1870-2020 below"

Sl No	Year	Denomination	Weight of the Coin	Metal Compositions	Shape & Size			Mint
					Dia	Edge	Shape	
1	2021	100 Rupees	35 G	Quaternary Alloy	44 Mm	Milled	Circular	Kolkata

SHRI GURU TEGH BAHADUR JI (2022)

Date of Issue: 21st APRIL 2022

OBVERSE DESCRIPTION OF COIN

Ashoka Lion Capital Denomination with Rupee Symbol Bharat /India on Sides

REVERSE DESCRIPTION OF COIN

Image of Gurudwara Guru Ka Mahal, Amritsar with two swords are encompassing with year 1621-2021 below the image,Legend "400th Birth Anniversary of Sri Guru Tegh Bahadur Ji" in English and Hindi.,Legends in Punjabi are also visible

SI No	Year	Denomination	Weight of the Coin	Metal Compositions	Shape & Size			Mint
					Dia	Edge	Shape	
1	2021	400 Rupees	35	Quaternary Alloy	44 Mm	Milled	Circular	Mumbai

UNIVERSITY OF DELHI

Date of Issue: 1ˢᵗ MAY 2022

OBVERSE DESCRIPTION OF COIN
Ashoka Lion Capital Denomination with Rupee Symbol Bharat /India on Sides

REVERSE DESCRIPTION OF COIN
Logo of "University of Delhi" with the year "2022",Legend "Centenary Year of University of Delhi" in English and Hindi.

Sl No	Year	Denomina-tion	Weight of the Coin	Metal Com-positions	Shape & Size			Mint
					Dia	Edge	Shape	
1	2021	125 Rupees	35g	Silver	44 Mm	Milled With 200 Serra-tions	Round	Kolkata

75th YEAR OF INDEPENDENCE (AZADI KA AMRIT MAHOSTAV)

Date of Issue: 06th JUNE 2022

OBVERSE DESCRIPTION OF COIN
Ashoka Lion Capital Denomination with Rupee Symbol Bharat /India on Sides

REVERSE DESCRIPTION OF COIN
Logo of Azadi Ka amrit Mahostavat the center, Legend "75th year of Independence" with year mentioned at the left center, Denomination with rupees symbol.

SI No	Year	Denomination	Weight of the Coin	Metal Compositions	Shape & Size			Mint
					Dia	Edge	Shape	
1	2022	1 Rupees	3.09 Gms	Ferritic Ss	20 Mm	Milled	Circular	Mumbai
2	2022	2 Rupees	4.07 Gms	Ferritic Ss	23 Mm	Milled	Circular	Mumbai
3	2022	5 Rupees	6.74 Gms	Nickel Brass	25 Mm	Milled	Circular	Mumbai
4	2022	10 Rupees	7.74 Gms	Bio Mattric	27 Mm	Milled	Circular	Mumbai
5	2022	20 Rupees	8.54 Gms	Bio Mattric	27 Mm	Milled	Dedecagon	Mumbai

SRIMAT SWAMI PRANAVANDADJI MAHARAJ

Date of Issue: 27th July 2022

OBVERSE DESCRIPTION OF COIN

Ashoka Lion Capital Denomination with Rupee Symbol Bharat /India on Sides

REVERSE DESCRIPTION OF COIN

Portrait of Srimat Swami Pranavanandji Maharaj, Legend "125th Birth Anniversary Year of Srimat Swami Pranavanandji Maharaj" with year 2021 below.

Sl No	Year	Denomina-tion	Weight of the Coin	Metal Com-positions	Shape & Size			Mint
					Dia	Edge	Shape	
1	2022	10 Rupees	7.74 Gms	Bi-Metallic	27 Mm	Milled	Circlur	Kolkata
2	2022	50 Rupees	22.5 Gms	Quaternary Alloy	39 Mm	Milled	Circlur	Kolkata
3	2022	100 Rupess	356 Gms	Quaternary Alloy	44 Mm	Milled	Circlur	Kolkata